The Nature of
Florida's Beaches
Including
Sea Beans, Laughing Gulls and Mermaids' Purses

by Cathie Katz

Other books by Cathie Katz

The Nature of Florida's Waterways
Including Dragonflies, Cattails and Mangrove Snapper

The Nature of Florida's Neighborhoods
Including Bats, Scrub Jays, Lizards and Wildflowers

The Nature of Florida's Ocean Life
Including Coral Reefs, Gulf Stream, Sargasso Sea and Sunken Ships

Nature a Day at a Time:
An Uncommon Look at Common Wildlife

The Nature of Florida's
Beaches

Including

Sea Beans, Laughing Gulls
and
Mermaids' Purses

Written and Illustrated by Cathie Katz

Great Outdoors Publishing Co.

The Nature of Florida's Beaches
Including Sea Beans, Laughing Gulls and Mermaids' Purses

First Printing 1995, 2nd Printing 1995, 3rd Printing 1998, 4th Printing 2001, 5th Printing 2007

Published by:
Great Outdoors Publishing Company, Inc.
www.floridabooks.com

The information about edibles in this book is general. Any plant or marine substance used externally or internally can cause allergic reactions in some people. Neither the publisher nor the author accept responsibility for any harm resulting from mistaken identity or inappropriate use of any wild edible.

Publisher's Cataloging-in-Publication Data

Katz, Cathie
    The Nature of Florida's Beaches Including Sea Beans, Laughing Gulls and Mermaids' Purses / by Cathie Katz.
    Includes bibliographic references and index.
    LCCN: 2001091071
    ISBN: 0-8200-1201-7

    1. Seashore biology–Florida. 2. Natural history–Florida. 3. Marine invertebrates–Florida. 4. Coastal flora–Florida. 5. Seeds–Tropics. 6. Sea turtles–Florida. I. Title.

574.526.38

Printed in the United States of America.

The Nature of
Florida's Beaches

Including
Sea Beans, Laughing Gulls and Mermaids' Purses

Written and Illustrated by

Cathie Katz

WAVES
A rush … then a hush …
A rumble … then a tumble …
the waves roll up
to the sand;

A treasure of shells
arrives with each crest,
as the sea gives gifts
to the land.

—Patricia Ryan Frazier © 1998

The Nature of Florida's Beaches

CONTENTS

The Nature of Florida's Beaches

INTRODUCTION

When I moved to Melbourne Beach in 1983, 1 kept finding strange things on the beach that I couldn't identify…

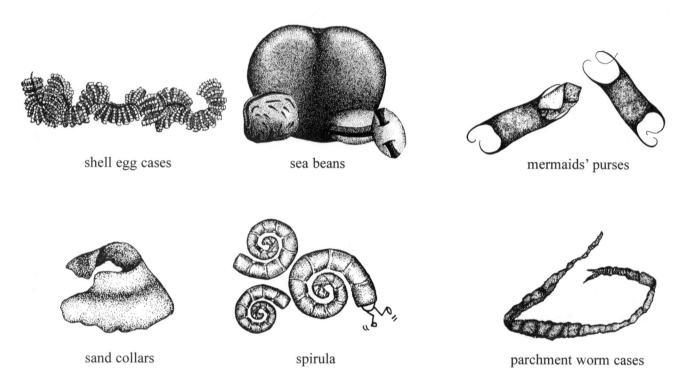

shell egg cases   sea beans   mermaids' purses

sand collars   spirula   parchment worm cases

…and lots of other things that I had never seen before. To answer the question, "What is it?" I searched through shell guides, botany books, marine life dictionaries and fossil books. I also spoke with biologists and naturalists and eventually realized that a need existed to compile and share all the information I was gathering.

During this research, I began to see the beach as a habitat where all the things I found were related to each other and to our lives. I was struck by the connections to nature, history, geography, medicine and art. For example, when I started learning about sea beans, I discovered that Christopher Columbus studied the world's currents by watching sea beans drift in the ocean; that sea beans helped disperse plants to faraway continents; that they've been used as medicine for centuries, and they can be sprouted (they're alive!). I also learned the Central and South American rain forests are home to many of the sea beans found on Florida's coast.

In this booklet, I hope to convey an idea of this connectedness. This is the first in a series of four books about Florida's habitats.

Sea Beans, Laughing Gulls and Mermaids' Purses

In this book, I focused on the common-but-hard-to-identify beach treasures found in Florida. I didn't cover all the shells and birds and fish in Florida since that is beyond the scope of this book. Lots of specific field guides are available to help with those identifications; some of those guides are listed in the bibliography.

I devoted six full pages to describe sea beans because, for me (and others with sea bean fever), they are the best of all beach treasures… they're magical and exotic… and they were the most difficult for me to research. Whenever I asked about sea beans, the only reply I heard was "They bring good luck." When I finally discovered *World Guide to Tropical Drift Seeds and Fruits* by Charles R. Gunn and John V. Dennis, I knew I had found the mother lode of sea bean information! Almost everything I know about sea beans is based on this wonderful book (reprinted in 1999 by Krieger Publishing Co., Inc). When I met Dr. Gunn in Annapolis years after discovering his book, not only did I find a kindred spirit, I also found a friend whose enthusiasm for drift seeds inspired me and other beachcombers worldwide. A newsletter, *The Drifting Seed*, resulted from our mutual interest and curiosity about sea beans. The triannual newsletter connects people from more than 20 countries… all these connections just from picking up strange brown blobby things on the beach! Good luck for sure!

If you have questions or comments,
or are interested in knowing more about
The Drifting Seed newsletter, email your
comments and questions to
seabean@seabean.com

I have sat upon a trunk filled with diamonds and I have had my hands full of them, but… I have never seen jewels of earth to compare with the treasures the tides prodigally spill upon our beach: shells of pearl, fans of coral, angels' wings, and living stars. No shopping for man-made merchandise is as rewarding to me as combing god's bargain counter where collector's items are flung at my feet by the waves, without a penny to pay.
—Julia Lake Kellersberger, *Rooted in Florida Soil*

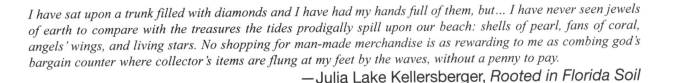

I was brainstorming with my friend Sue Kornbluh at a writers' conference in St. Petersburg in February 1995 when she suggested I add some character to my writing to liven it up. At that moment, a goofy little character barged into my work, running, dancing, laughing and playing on every page… usually inappropriately.

Her name is Little Larry and she's a creative spirit just like her namesake, Larry McGrath, whose spirit was with us that weekend. Before Larry passed away in January, he showed us by example how much fun the creative process could be. He sketched, wrote, painted and recited because he loved it all. No other reason.

I wrote this book with that feeling of fun that Larry inspired.

Beaches

The following pages describe the treasures you'll find in the sea wrack, the beach area, along the shore and in the dunes.

THE SEA WRACK

THE MORE YOU LOOK, THE MORE YOU SEE.

Always, then, in this flotsam and jetsam of the tide lines, we are reminded that a strange and different world lies offshore. Though what we see here may be but the husks and fragments of life, through it we are made aware of life and death, of movement and change, of the transport of living things by tides, by wind-driven waves.

—Rachel Carson, *The Edge of the Sea*

The *SEA WRACK*: What is it? What's in it?

A wrack is the strip of seaweed and ocean debris left on the beach by the high tides.

← *Sargassum weed, shells, turtle grass, shell egg cases, barnacles, mermaids' purses, sea beans, spirula, fossils, feathers, lava bomblets, sea lace, pumice, coral, sponges, beach glass, bones, opercula.*

In the winter, the wrack changes constantly with the wild tides, but during the summer, when tides are gentler, it lies undisturbed for months, drying out until the first stormy tides add more debris or wash it back out to the ocean.

"Eeeeuuuwww! Look at that junk!"

mermaid's purse

spirula

When I hear people complain about the seaweed messing up the beach, I want to shout, "It's not junk! Look! It's filled with treasures and clues about life in the ocean millions of years ago!"

sea beans

ruddy turnstone

crucifix fish

gafftopsail catfish

ghost crab

To visit Florida's beaches without noticing the wrack is like driving to Disney World to admire its parking lot.

What is sargassum?

Sargassum (*Sargassum natans*) is seaweed, but different from seaweed or algae as we typically think of it… not the kind we eat with sushi. Sargassum comes from a giant free-floating bed of vegetation that drifts over thousands of miles in the Sargasso Sea in the middle of the Atlantic Ocean. This undulating prairie weighs thousands of tons, but is kept afloat by millions of little air sacs that grow among the leaves and stems.

Those little brown balls that we see rolling around the beach are the air sacs from the sargassum.

A ring of currents in the middle of the Atlantic Ocean encloses a giant eddy which rotates clockwise. Clumps of sargassum accumulate in this swirling, powerful eddy, picking up and tossing out marine creatures and objects from other continents that eventually wash up on our beach.

When Columbus saw the huge mass of seaweed he thought he was near land. Actually he was only halfway across the Atlantic.

An entry in the *Santa Maria's* log, September 17, 1492:

The ship drifts on, though there is no wind. The sea is covered with dense weed so far as one can see, and looking like green ice. A whale is sighted. The air is light. The sea is so warm that the sailors undress and go swimming amongst the weed.

How does sargassum grow if it's not in soil?

Sargassum weed reproduces itself on the ocean's surface, nourished by marine creatures living in it and by unlimited sunshine and moisture. Researchers are still wondering how this free-floating mass (as large as the United States) found its way to create a new habitat in the middle of the ocean.

"Once they were at home [sargassum creatures] *close to rocky and coral shores, when the tides washed in and out and they were able to leave the weed and go searching for food in the crevices of the reefs. Then one stormy day, the weed was torn loose from its foothold, and its occupants, involuntary passengers, found themselves adrift in the ocean in totally new surroundings."*

—Marjory Bartlett Sanger, *The World of the Great White Heron*

Camouflage Masters

Incredible sea creatures live in this seaweed and can imitate the colors, shapes and textures of sargassum leaves, stems and air sacs. If you look closely at the clumps of seaweed on our beach, you might see a crab, shrimp, fish, seahorse or worm found only in sargassum weed.

↗ The **sargassum fish** (*Histrio histrio*) is the master of camouflage. It spends its entire life in the weeds. Its fins mimic branches and leaves, its mottled coloring blends with the lumpy sargassum, and even the white spots on its body look like the encrustations (bryozoans) that grow on sargassum. It "climbs" around the sargassum weed, luring smaller fish toward its mouth by using a fishing pole that's attached to its snout.

When we're faced with unexpected changes in living conditions, we can either adapt or perish. If we choose to adapt, we become stronger after the struggle. Over hundreds of thousands of years the sargassum creatures evolved into remarkable survivors by adapting to their weed-home in color, shape and design.

Seaweed World

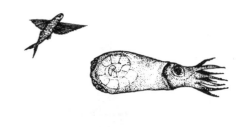

Underneath the sargassum, the sea is more than 4 miles deep! Creatures who live in this weed community must hang on tight or else disappear into the dark abyss. **Flying fish** (*Hirundichthys affinis*) use a sticky substance to attach strings of eggs onto the weed. The newly hatched fish (called fry) stay in between the leaves until they're strong enough to survive in the ocean.

Flying fish use their tails like outboard motors to propel them out of water where they then "fly" at 35 miles per hour.

Spirula or **ram's horn shell** (*Spirula spirula*) is the inside structure of a squid that lives in the depths of the Sargasso Sea. We see the delicate spiral shell on our beach in the fall, but rarely see the squid itself. When this tiny squid dies, the gas-filled chambered shell floats to the surface where it drifts with the sargassum and the currents for thousands of miles before it reaches our coast.

↗ **Sargassum crabs** (*Portunus sayi*) and **gulfweed shrimp** (*Latreutes fucorum*) are tiny yellow-brown sea creatures entirely dependent on the sargassum community. ↓

↗ Agile and beautiful **seahorses** (*Hippocampus* sp.) can hang onto weeds with their tails. Their pectoral fins work like little propellers, fluttering as fast as 70 times each second. During courtship, the female pursues the mate in an elaborate wooing dance where she swims in circles around him. At the end of the dance they meet in an embrace and she transfers her eggs to his pouch. Male seahorses carry the eggs in their pouches and when a pony (a young seahorse) is ready to leave Dad, it's no bigger than a piece of a Cheerio.

Thus the Sargasso is a sea of disguises which reveal all too clearly the fierce, predatory competition for existence in a region where once only doldrums were thought to prevail.
—Marjory Bartlett Sanger, *The World of the Great White Heron*

Where in the world do these things come from?

The **pumice** that we find on our beach is lightweight volcanic material from lava that floated to the ocean's surface and traveled with the currents for thousands of miles. ↓

← These popcorn-sized orange balls are called **lava bomblets** and are probably volcanic froth from lava emissions. Even lighter than pumice, they float onto the beach with the sargassum once in awhile in the winter.

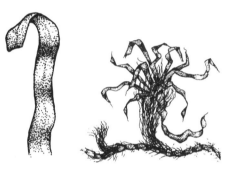

Mixed in with the wrack is **turtle grass** ↑ (*Thalassia testudinum*) which grows over shallow bottoms unlike the free-floating sargassum. This seed-bearing plant is actually a grass, not a seaweed, and it has beautiful blooms. When the leaves and flowers dry out in the wrack, the ribbon-like clusters can be used in artwork and dried flower arrangements. ↗

Bubble bath?

← The fluffy balls of foam that we see rolling around the beach on windy days are evidence of the ocean's cleaning methods. Tiny bits of debris dissolve in the ocean and act as soapy cleansing agents.

The mysterious oil blob fish:

"All the flotsam and jetsam of the ocean—drifting tree trunks, boxes, light-bulbs—quickly become the encrusted homes of small oceanic animals. But the most extraordinary of these microscopic island havens on the shelterless plains of the ocean are blobs of fuel oil, which become populated not only with barnacles and hydroids and egg-laying Halobates but, most remarkably, with a small fish which almost exactly resembles the oil blob in both shape and color. Since fuel oil has been floating on the oceans of the world for only about forty-five years, this fish cannot have evolved this resemblance in so short a period... All that one can say is that this 'oilfish' may have selected its new home shrewdly, for a predator that had previously encountered oil might be wary of attacking any object simulating it."

—Richard Perry, The Unknown Ocean

11

Off Base Housing

Horseshoe crabs (*Limulus polyphemus*) are relics of a group of creatures (related to spiders) that existed more than half a billion years ago. They look dangerous with that thorny hard armor, but they're harmless. They can't bite or sting and the mean-looking stinger is only used for balance and to right themselves when they are thrown on their backs.

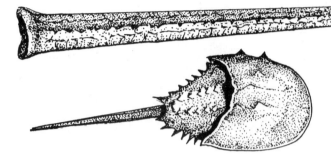

Even though we don't get to see the horseshoe crabs' famous mass mating ritual, we see evidence of it when we find their long tail spikes and broken armament pieces washed up with the early summer tides.

A horseshoe crab must walk to eat… if it stops walking, it can't eat. Its mouth is on the bottom of its body and surrounded by "knees" that cause the teeth to grind while the crab is walking.

Horseshoe crabs are edible but the little bit of meat inside is barely worth the cleaning effort.

← Occasionally, **sponges** reach our shores. Those sponges are actually the skeletons of marine animals. The holes are pores used for breathing and eating. Sponges hatch from eggs. After they're born, they latch onto any object in the ocean and continue to grow about an inch a year.

Those clusters of tiny holes that we see in shells were probably made by boring sponges eating away at the shell. ↙

↘

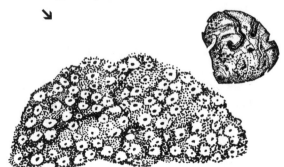

↗ Like sponges, corals are actually the skeletons of colonies of animals that secrete a hard lime substance in which they live. The animals are carnivorous and eat sea urchin eggs, shrimp embryo and tiny jellyfish. I find broken parts of coral skeletons mixed in with the sea wrack throughout the year.

Barnacles

A **barnacle** spends its entire life upside down, anchored by its head to an object. It eats by kicking its feathery tentacles out of its hard interlocking plates, catching plankton in the sea soup around them.

We find about a dozen species of barnacles on our beach that have broken away from their home base. We can't always tell where they're from because they hitch rides on ships and floating bottles from all over the world.

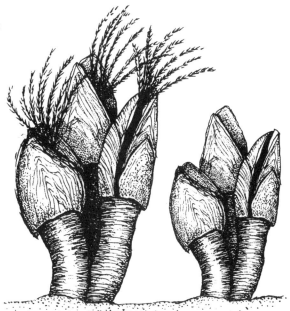

↗ **Common goose barnacle** (*Lepas anatifera*)

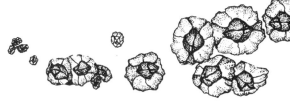

Inside the doors of the **little gray barnacle** ↖ ↗ (*Chthamalus fragilis*) is a little igloo-like house where the barnacle lives.

↘ **Acorn barnacles** (*Balanus balanoides*)

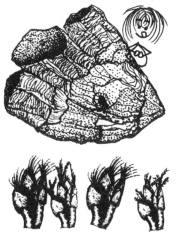

Some people eat the flesh of big barnacles which tastes like a blend of lobster and crab (*not chicken*).

The glue that barnacles use to anchor onto wet surfaces is the strongest ever known; dentists would like to copy it. Jack Rudloe, author of *The Erotic Ocean*, describes how his dentist friend grows barnacles on dead teeth by embedding the teeth in Styrofoam and floating them off a dock; later, the dentist removes the barnacle-encrusted teeth to study the secret secretions.

When I find newly washed up barnacles with their feathery legs waving in the air, I want to put them back in the sea to save their lives. I forget that their lives include being food for shore birds and crabs.

Odd Things

How do barnacles find mates when they're stuck in one place? They live in clusters and have long tubes that reach toward the closest neighbor—male or female, it doesn't matter since they all have both sex organs.

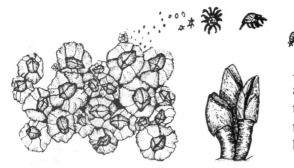

After barnacles hatch (from eggs), they go through an amazing transformation: From shrimp-like larvae they change from one-eyed six-legged creatures to two-eyed twelve-legged creatures, then they become blind crustaceans with feathery tentacles.

Charles Darwin was so fascinated with barnacles that he collected ten thousand (in his house) to classify and describe. His work is still used for reference.

Sometimes you'll find strange objects in the sea wrack that are hard to categorize. One of these objects is a white bony rattle. Because of the similarity to Christ on the cross, this structure is called a **crucifix fish**. It's from the skull of a **sailcat**. Legend says if you hear the dice being tossed when you shake it, you will be blessed.

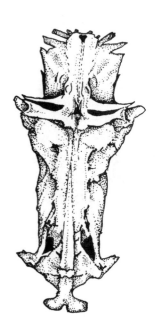

↗ A male **sailcat** or **gafftopsail catfish** (*Bagre marinus*) carries the eggs of the female sailcat in his mouth. Each egg is about ¾ inch and he can carry 50 in his mouth, not eating until they hatch. Even after they're born, they go back into his mouth for protection.

If you follow nature, you are not experimenting. Nature has done that for you long ago.
—John C. Gifford, *Living by the Land*

To and From the Sea

A **mermaid's purse** is the egg case of a **clearnose skate** (*Raja eglanteria*). The tiny skate develops inside the case the same way that a chick grows in an egg. After about nine weeks, a perfectly formed skate slips out, unfolding itself to start life in the ocean.

The sea wrack provides nutrients for shore birds like the **ruddy turnstone** (*Arenaria interpres*) whose name came from their habit of turning shells and stones over to find bits of food. Sometimes they're called calico-backs because of their patterned plumage in the summer. More appropriately, my mother calls them ready stone-turners.

Not only does the sargassum weed carry marine life in from the sea, it also helps carry sea creatures out to sea from the beach…

…**Sea turtle hatchlings**, just free from the restrictions of their underground nests, start life by energetically racing over the sand toward the surf. Exhausted by the time they reach the open sea, they use clumps of sargassum to carry them farther out to sea. The beds of sargassum provide the tiny sea turtles with nourishment, shelter and exploration activities. After entering the Gulf Stream, the young turtles swim eastward across the Atlantic, then south around the Sargasso Sea, then westward back to Florida's coast. They circle the Sargasso Sea many times before returning to their home area to nest several years later.

All these birds, insects, animals, reptiles, whistling, whispering, screaming, howling, croaking, fish in their kinds teeming, plants thrusting and struggling, life in its million, its billion forms, the greatest concentration of living things on this continent, they made up the first Florida.

—Marjory Stoneman Douglas, *Florida: The Long Frontier*

Sea Beans

What are they? Where do they come from?

Sea beans grow on tropical vines and trees from as far away as Africa, Australia, Asia, and South America. Most of the sea beans that we find on our coast come from Central and South American forests and Caribbean islands, but because of their durability and their ability to travel thousands of miles, it's difficult to determine their place of origin.

Sea beans fall from their parent plant into streams and rivers, such as the Amazon, and float out into ocean currents where they can drift for years until they wash onto a shore thousands of miles away.

Christopher Columbus and Charles Darwin used sea beans to study the oceans' currents. Benjamin Franklin made one of the first accurate maps of the Gulf Stream in 1770, but he didn't realize that it extended as far as the European coasts.

The Curse of the Coco-de-Mer:

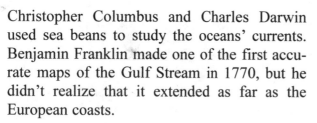

Death by firing squad? For a bean?! In past centuries, one particular sea bean, as big as a watermelon, was credited with almost supernatural properties. In the Seychelles where this coco-de-mer grows, a law stated that if you found one and didn't turn it in to the authorities, you would be killed by firing squad.

And here are seeds unnumbered, washed up from the tropics, sea beans—as they are called, several species and usually supposed to live in the ocean. Some of these are Mucunas, rank vines which grow in Cuba and other West Indian Islands, which bear large clusters of handsome flowers followed by black, rough pods filled with beans. I have gathered and planted hundreds of them and finally got one to grow.

—Charles Torrey Simpson, *Florida Wild Life*

Sea Beans

World Travelers

If you're lucky, you can watch a sea bean "armada" wash up with the first wild tides around the harvest moon. I've stood in the surf as they came rolling in and collected more than one hundred in one hour. Typically, though, I find one or two at a time higher up on the beach, closer to the wrack. Beans in the wrack may have been left from previous years. Sometimes you can see clues about how long they've been at sea or how long they've been on the beach: Notice if there are worms, algae, sea lace or barnacles stuck to them.

Those inconsequential white smudges on some sea beans are actually colonies of tiny animals called **sea lace** (Bryozoa), neatly arranged to form lacy patterns. Each animal is smaller than this apostrophe (☞'). The animals (*Membranipora tuberculata*) secrete a chemical which builds their hard "house."

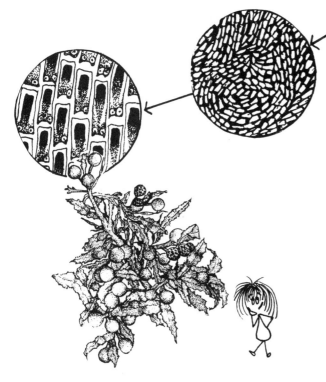

I never paid attention to these frosty spots, thinking they were bird poops, until I noticed that sometimes sea beans had the same spots that I saw on sargassum. I looked at the spots under a magnifying glass and was astounded at their intricate beauty. I learned that this particular design only grew in the Sargassum Sea. Does that mean the sea bean hitched a ride from South America by riding on the floating seaweed? Must be so.

I've found fewer sea beans these past few years and I wonder if the beans are missing because of rain forest development? That would be bad news since rain forest plants have been studied to cure diseases such as melanoma and leukemia. Drugs from some of the forest plants have already been successfully used to treat Hodgkin's disease, hypertension and rheumatoid arthritis. Sea beans have been used medicinally for centuries. Who knows what other potential cures are hidden within these exotic seeds?

...the Amazon forest contains a third of the planet's trees and supplies half its oxygen. Getting rid of what is in essence the planet's lungs has an impact way beyond Brazil's borders.
—Kenneth C. Davis, *Don't Know Much About Geography*

17

Sea Bean Season

Florida's beaches are wonderful for finding lots of different sea beans. The Gulf Stream carries more than 100 species of sea beans to Florida's beaches, usually in the fall after high tides. The number of beans you can find in a day will vary with time of year, Gulf Stream quirks, offshore hurricane activity, wind and temperature changes, and jungle plant abundance for a particular year. And naturally, early morning beachcombers will have better luck, especially after a late night high tide.

Florida's coast is a combination of transition zones where water changes from subtropical to tropical to temperate temperatures. Heading north, the Gulf Stream veers dramatically away from the Eastern Shore, and wave action is much greater than in the south because of the Bahama Platform (a geological shelf that subdues South Florida's waves).

Seeing the first clumps of seaweed at the beginning of autumn is a good sign that sea beans are on their way. The drifting seeds probably get caught in the floating patches of weed at the edge of the Sargasso Sea; the seeds either spin away from the giant bed of vegetation to drift to Holland, Ireland, England and maybe Florida… or they are pulled toward the center to travel with the Sargassum for a few years while collecting marine algae, barnacles and sea lace.

Can You Grow Sea Beans?

You can sprout sea beans, but keeping them alive outside in our cool winter climate is difficult. If you can keep them inside (away from temperatures below 50°F) they will survive, but most of them grow so fast that they can easily take over your home.

To grow, they must be cracked open or a hole must be drilled through the hard shell so fresh water can reach the seed. After a few days the bean will swell and then sprout. (Since some beans don't have a viable seed inside, you may need to try a few at a time.) Put the sprouted seed in good potting soil and continue watering.

The seeds inside some beans can remain alive for hundreds of years. One unusual sea bean was discovered in an Egyptian tomb, more than 2000 years old… when the bean was exposed to humid air, it grew into an orchid that was thought to be extinct.

Some of the most interesting beans that we find are the sea heart, sea purse, sea pearl, Mary's bean, starnut palm, sea coconut, and the true sea bean (hamburger bean).

↗ The most familiar drift seed is the **true sea bean** or hamburger bean (*Mucuna* spp.) There are several of this species, varying slightly in color and shape, but most look like little hamburgers.

↗ The **sea purse** (*Dioclea reflexa*) is one of the prettiest sea beans; some have black swirls on an orange background and others are a solid yellow-gold. Most of them are shinier than the true sea bean, and the *hilum* (the band that surrounds most of the edge) is generally narrower than the true sea bean's hilum.

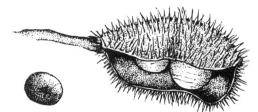

A few hundred years ago, the ↑ **sea pearl** or nickernut (*Caesalpinia bonduc*) was worn attached to string around the neck as an amulet to ward off the Evil Eye. (More about sea pearls on page 55.)

↙ The **sea heart** (*Entada gigas*) supposedly inspired Columbus to find new land in the west. In the Azores, the sea heart is called *fava de Colón* (Columbus bean). The Gulf Stream carried sea hearts to northern European beaches where they were commonly made into snuff boxes by polishing them and cutting them in half and attaching little hinges.

Sea hearts grow in long three-foot flat pods. In the rain forests, sea heart lianas twine through the forest canopy. The vine is called *escalera de mono* (monkey ladder) because it gives the monkeys a maze of connected ladders for transportation.

Sea Beans

Bay bean vines grow all over Florida's dunes, so we find their beans almost all year. Similarly, mangrove pods wash onto the beach frequently because of the abundance of nearby mangrove islands. Our bay beans (see Page 59) and mangrove pods float from our waterways to the Gulf Stream and then travel to other beaches and perhaps other continents.

↗ **Bay beans** (*Canavalia rosea*) have a potential to help cure cancer since the seeds contain *concanavaline A*, which affects blood cells and certain tumor cells.

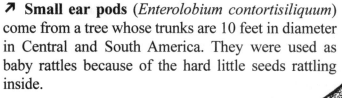

↗ **Small ear pods** (*Enterolobium contortisiliquum*) come from a tree whose trunks are 10 feet in diameter in Central and South America. They were used as baby rattles because of the hard little seeds rattling inside.

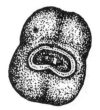
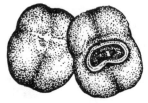

Mary's bean ↖↗ (*Merremia discoidesperma*) is also known as the crucifix bean because of the cross indented across both sides. They grow in papery capsules on tropical climbing vines in several tropical areas of the world.

Starnut palms ↗ (*Astrocaryum huicungo*) vary in size and shape, but always have little holes at their base like bowling bowls, placed between swirling lines.

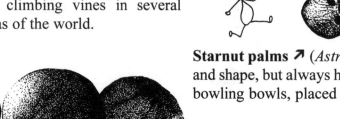

The **sea coconut** ↖↗ (*Manicaria saccifera*) ↖→ is one of the most plentiful of all sea beans on East Florida's coast. We see the dumpling-sized brown balls rolling in the surf and sand, sometimes in clusters of three, still in their pods. The tree from which it grows has the largest leaf of any plant.

Country almonds, coconuts, mango seeds, box fruits, calabashes, locusts, mahogany pods and fern palms are just a few of the other drift seeds found on our beach.

Sea Bean Polishing

Sea beans can be polished to a high gloss by using sandpaper, a Dremel, a Cabochon machine or a rock tumbler. Hand sanding or using a Dremel is a slow, one-bean-at-a-time process because the outer shells of sea beans are so hard that it takes a lot of sanding before they get shiny. Cabochon machines are expensive and cumbersome, especially if you have limited space.

An easy, fun and inexpensive way to polish beans is by using a rock tumbler the same way you would use one to shine stones; you'll need to buy supplies from a lapidist's (stone expert's) shop: a rock tumbler, two grades of silicon grit (coarse and fine), ground walnut shells, polish and reactivator cream. (Jack the Lapidist in Melbourne helped me find these things and warned me that tumbling is a very slow process.)

↗ Sea hearts, true sea beans, sea pearls, sea purses and starnut palms are the best beans to polish because they have sturdy outer shells and will give a high shine.

In a rock tumbler, you can polish 50 to 100 at a time without having to do much. The beans need to be tumbled in a cup of coarse silicon grit (dry) for about 4 weeks (until they lose their coarseness), then in a fine grit for about 2 more weeks. They should be very smooth (but still dull) at this point and ready to be polished. Clean them well by tumbling for 10 minutes or so in soapy water or sand. (No particles of grit should be left on them). Then put in a clean tumbling bowl with ground walnut shells mixed with 2 tablespoons of good polish (such as optimum cerium oxide) with a few drops of reactivator cream (or furniture polish or high-gloss car wax).

I experimented with different amounts and types of grits and polishing agents for a long time, fumbling along the way. You might come up with a better and faster way by experimenting with other substances. I had to visit Jack the Lapidist many times for advice before I was able to see some good results, and now I can polish sea beans to a sparkling glossy shine.

Sea hearts, which have a much softer outer shell than the other beans, can be polished in two or three days in a rock tumbler without going through the grit phase, but each seed must be completely free of debris before polishing. Sea pearls (nickernuts) are so smooth naturally, you can shine them in a day by just tumbling in the polishing phase.

The oceans of the world are restless and, in addition to their regular tidal movements, they flow in definite paths across the earth. Any object—even a seed—that falls into the ocean may be transported a long way and eventually washed up on some foreign share, If one studies the distribution of the world's vegetation it becomes obvious that ocean currents have had much to do with plant geography. It is believed, for example, that the original home of the coconut palm was the western coast of Central America, but ocean currents, long ago, carried floating coconuts to almost every continent and island where they could possibly germinate and grow.

—Ross E. Hutchins, *The Amazing Seeds*

THE BEACH

At one time beachcombing was more than just a hobby or a pleasant form of exercise. Many years ago when those of us who lived near the sea needed chairs for our homes, pots and pans for our kitchen, or even clothes for ourselves and our families, we first scoured the beach, hoping that we might find them there. If we came back empty-handed, we reluctantly took down the mail order catalogs and sent away for the articles. But buying was never as much fun as finding!

—John C. Gifford, *Living by the Land*

Where do shells come from?

The shells that we find on our beach are the discarded "houses" of soft marine animals called mollusks. The word *mollusk* comes from a Latin word meaning *soft*.

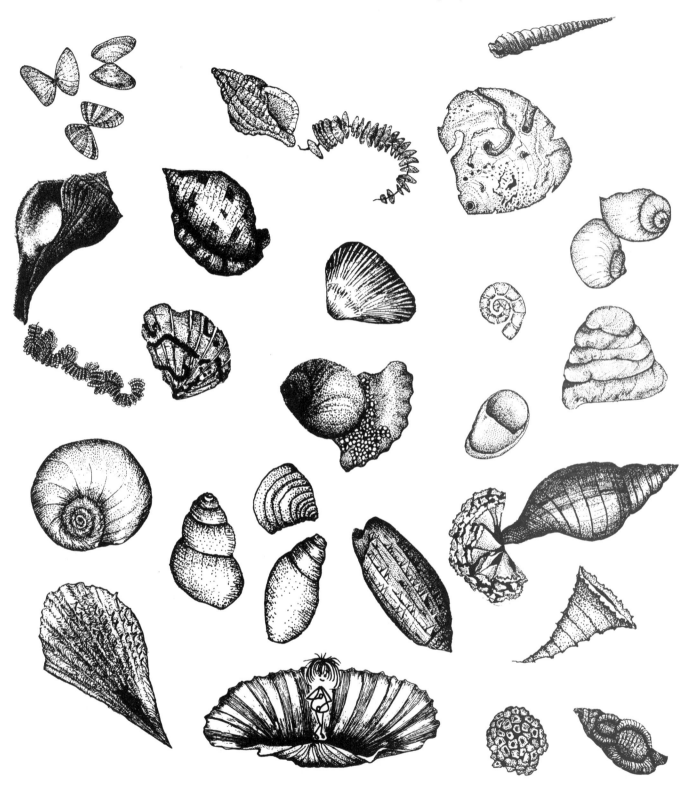

It is perhaps a more fortunate destiny to have a taste for collecting shells than to be born a millionaire.
—Robert Lewis Stevenson

Shell Egg Cases

Mollusks come from eggs that the female lays in clusters. Some of these eggs are laid in strong flexible casings for protection. The shell cases we find washed up on our beach are usually empty because the tiny mollusks already hatched at sea. Sometimes the perfectly formed miniature shells are still inside the parchment-like cases.

↙ The egg cases of the **common whelk** (*Buccinum undatum*) are called "sea wash balls" because sailors used them to wash their hands, claiming they produced a soapy lather. These egg cases wash up on our beach after the summer egg laying. The adult common whelk is the edible "snail" that Europeans eat.

A **moon snail** (*Polinices duplicatus*) → makes a flexible collar out of sand mixed with a chemical secretion to protect her eggs, which she lays inside the collar. These collars will dry out and crumble as soon as they're away from water. If you want to preserve one, soak it in an alcohol and glycerine mixture or spray with lacquer.

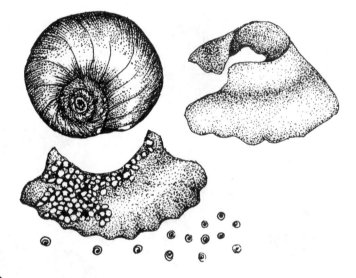

← **Channeled whelks'** (*Busycon canaliculatum*) egg cases are flat disks strung together, each pillow-like disk filled with about 50 miniature whelks. They develop for about two months before hatching.

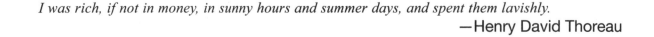

I was rich, if not in money, in sunny hours and summer days, and spent them lavishly.
—Henry David Thoreau

Shell Egg Cases

The egg case of the **knobbed whelk** ↘ (*Busycon carica*) is similar to the channeled whelk but each disk is wider with sharp ridges on the sides.

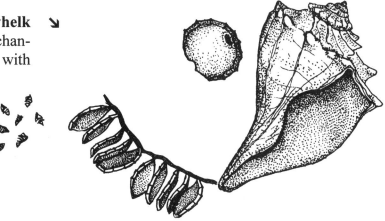

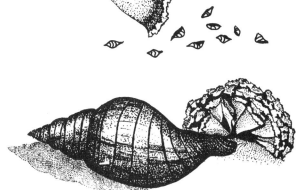

Only a few young **banded tulips** (*Fasciolaria hunteria*) survive because as soon as they break out of their egg cases, they begin eating each other. Tulips are the most aggressive and cannibalistic of all Florida mollusks.

Oddly, tulip shell egg cases look a lot like a sponge (*Neoesperiopsis digitata*) found on beaches in Alaska. Why would that be?

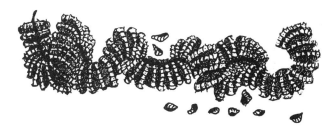

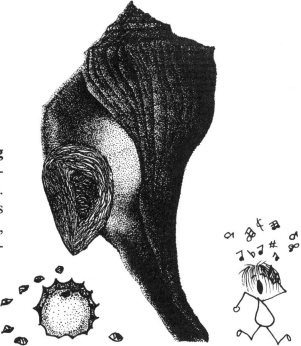

The egg cases ↑ of the **left-handed** or **lightning whelk** (*Busycon contrarium*) are the most common of the egg cases found on Florida's beaches. The shell of the lightning whelk is almost always left-handed; when you hold one up by the thin end, the opening is on the left. Why is this shell left-handed when all other univalves are right-handed?

← The **operculum** is the trapdoor that the mollusk uses to seal out the rest of the world. *Operculum* comes from the Latin word for lid or cover.

Shell Shocked

When we find an empty shell, it's easy to forget that a complex animal with intestines, mouth, heart and kidneys once lived inside the shell. When the animal is eaten by a predator, the empty shell will eventually wash up onto a beach. Most shells give us clues about mollusk activity if we examine the burrows, holes and breaks.

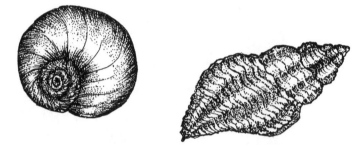

A neat beveled hole near the hinge was probably drilled by a **moon snail** → (*Polinices*) to get to the flesh. It drills through the hard shell with file-like teeth and an acid secretion produced by a special gland. It can drill a hole in 10 minutes.

A tiny straight hole is usually done by the filing of an **Atlantic oyster drill** ↗ (*Urosalpinx cinerea*).

← **Marine worms** (*Vericularia*) can leave distinct evidence by their squiggly secretions.

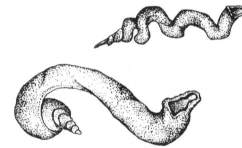

No markings on a shell might mean that a human or a **whelk** ate it. A whelk grabs its victim with a muscular foot and hangs on while banging its own shell against the edge until it breaks. Then the whelk sticks its snout into the break and cuts the meat, twisting it out. →

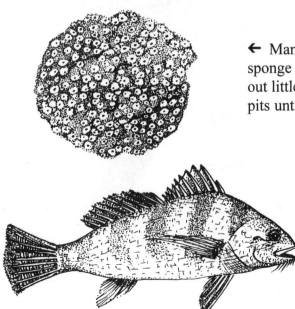

← Many tiny holes close together are made by a boring sponge (*Cliona*). The sponge secretes a chemical that eats out little pits in the shell. It will riddle the shell with these pits until the mollusk weakens and dies.

The **black drum** (*Pogonias cromis*) grinds up shellfish with a powerful crushing structure in its throat, swallowing the meat and spitting out the pieces of shell.

Walking on History

Whenever we walk on Florida's parking lots, boat ramps and beaches, we're walking on millions of years of history. Ancient shells can be found all over Florida because the peninsula was under the sea millions of years ago. The rises and falls of the sea level left behind fossils 100 thousand to 50 million years ago. In shell fossils, we see similarities to the mollusks that exist today.

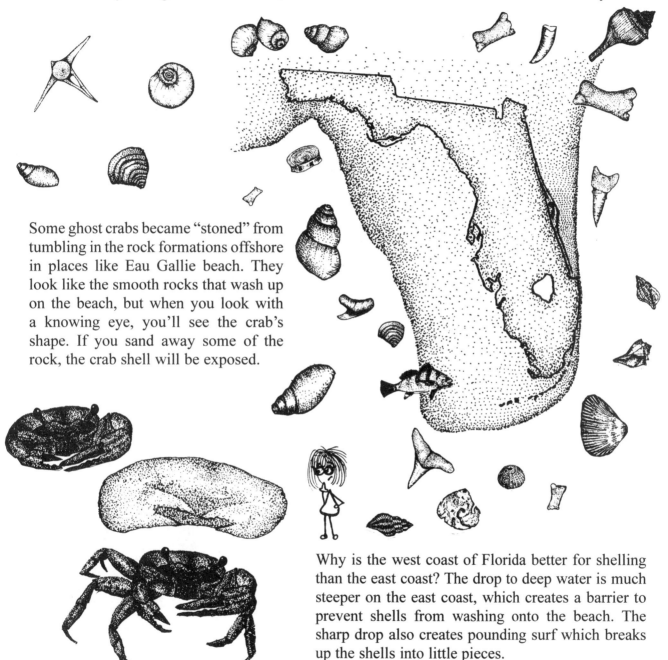

Some ghost crabs became "stoned" from tumbling in the rock formations offshore in places like Eau Gallie beach. They look like the smooth rocks that wash up on the beach, but when you look with a knowing eye, you'll see the crab's shape. If you sand away some of the rock, the crab shell will be exposed.

Why is the west coast of Florida better for shelling than the east coast? The drop to deep water is much steeper on the east coast, which creates a barrier to prevent shells from washing onto the beach. The sharp drop also creates pounding surf which breaks up the shells into little pieces.

Higher than normal tides occur around full and new moons. When storms combine with these high tides, treasures from sunken ships are carried to shore with the ocean debris. Spanish ships headed for Florida between the 16th and 18th centuries didn't always make it and their cargo is still being picked up on Florida's coast. Coins have been on the ocean bottom so long they've become encrusted, like the ghost crabs mentioned above, and are unrecognizable except by their shape: Large coins were divided up into eight pie-shaped segments ("pieces of eight") so they're somewhat triangular.

More Shells

The sturdy **quahog** (*Mercenaria mercenaria*) with its swirling purple designs was used to make wampum; the shells were broken, filed and drilled to make quarter-inch beads. The beads were strung or woven into belts. *Qua-hog* comes from Indian words meaning dark (or closed) and shell. ↓ ↘

The quahogs that we find on the beach are the shells discarded by surf anglers who use the meat for bait.

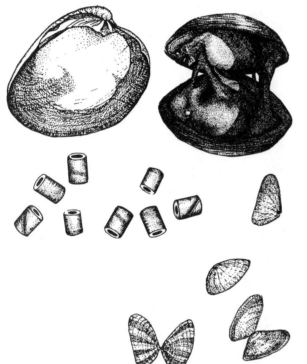

Tiny holes bubbling at the shore line are from the little butterfly-shaped pastel **coquinas** (*Donax variabilis*). If you scoop one up and look closely, you can see two siphon tubes coming from inside; one takes in water, the other expels it after oxygen and food are removed (filter feeding).

↙ If you scoop enough coquinas, you can make coquina soup: Make a broth by boiling the tiny clams (after rinsing them well), simmer for 20 minutes and strain the juice. Add potatoes, onions, celery and whatever else you have in your kitchen.

Four hundred years ago, the Spanish fort at St. Augustine was built from coquina rock. The rock is made from accumulations of these tiny shells.

The **calico scallop** (*Argopecten gibbus*) is one of the prettiest and most colorful shells on our beach, with yellows and pinks dominating. They are more plentiful than bay scallops, so what we order in restaurants are usually calico scallops. →

Calico scallops can open and close their shells so fast when they're in the sea that they can propel themselves away from predators such as starfish.

Most mollusks are blind, but calico scallops have two rows of iridescent turquoise eyes lining the edges of their shells, complete with cornea, lens and retina.

If I were to find only one calico scallop in my life, I would cherish it like a jewel. Unfortunately, I find lots of them.

We've got some bivalves!

Powerful muscles hold the shells of bivalves together. Bivalves are two-shelled mollusks like clams and coquinas. Pen shells are the biggest bivalves on Florida's beaches. The **saw-toothed pen shell** (*Atrina serrata*) produces black pearls, but I've never found one. **Stiff pen shells →** (*Atrina rigida*) are harvested for their adductor muscles and sold as scallops in some places.

Researchers discovered that pen shells have an amazing resistance to cancer.

Pen shells attach themselves to rocks in shallow water with an anchor called a *byssus* made of flexible threads. The byssus also picks up bits of other shells to help keep them anchored. In ancient times, the byssal threads were woven into fabric and may have been the legendary golden fleece. ↘

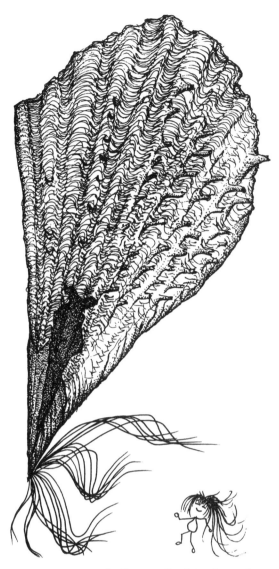

← One of the most common shells we find is the ark, a type of clam. The **ponderous ark** (*Noetia ponderosa*) has a black mossy coating. I always thought the black stuff was tar but it's actually part of the shell, used for camouflage. As it tumbles in the water and sand, the *periostracum* wears away and you can see how very white the ark really is.

Slipper shells (*Crepidula fornicata*) stack on top of each other with the males always on top. During mating, the male's sex organ reaches below to the lower shells. When the female on the bottom dies, the male above changes his sex to female, so a female is always on the bottom. Changing sexual orientation at some point in life is not unusual in the animal kingdom and also occurs in species such as sea bass and snook.

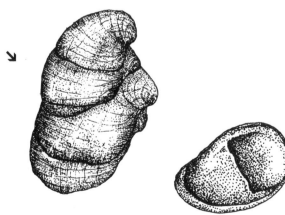

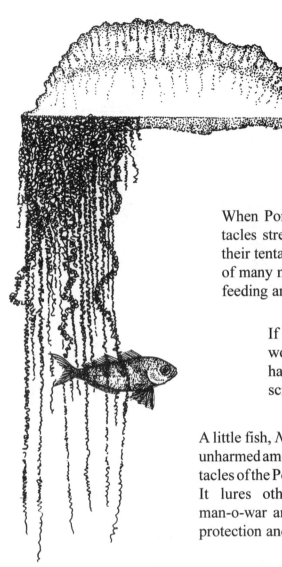

Jellyfish

The **Portuguese-man-o-war** (*Physalia physalia*) is a completely passive drifter whose tentacles extend more than 100 feet. Even after it dies, its long tentacles can still leave welts from a poison similar to cobra venom. Each tentacle has hundreds of tiny stinging cells (nematocysts). These cells have hair triggers; when they touch your skin, they explode, driving the venom-carrying threads into your flesh.

When Portuguese-men-o-war are out in the Gulf Stream, their tentacles stretch down to stun passing fish and they reel them in with their tentacles like skilled anglers. The tentacles are actually a colony of many marine animals, each with a different function: reproduction, feeding and protection.

If you get stung, pour ocean water, not fresh water, over the wounded area, then cover with any absorbent substance on hand—baking soda, flour, shaving cream… then carefully scrape it all away and wash again with ocean water.

A little fish, *Nomeus gronovii*, lives unharmed among the dangerous tentacles of the Portuguese-man-o-war. It lures other fish toward the man-o-war and in return, receives protection and fragments of food.

Peanut butter and jellyfish sandwich?

The **cannonball jellyfish** (*Stomolophus* ↘ *meleagris*) can be eaten as a snack (fried) or as a side dish. It's low in fat and cholesterol, and like tofu, it absorbs the flavors of whatever you cook with it. Lots of them wash up on the beach with seaweed.

Sometimes surfers or bathers think they've been stung by a Portuguese-man-o-war, but when it happens fast and jellyfish aren't in sight, it's probably the dreaded **sea wasp** (*Chiropsalmus quadrumanus*), also known as a box jellyfish.

Letting Go

Another common jellyfish in Florida is the **by-the-wind-sailor** (*Velella velella*). This polyp has a translucent bluish-purple raft with a flexible sail. Scientific references say these creatures have a sail "to let them tack with the wind," implying they can control their destination. Do they "tack" so they can wash up on our beach and die? It seems they just go where the wind takes them.

About half of them are "left-handed"... their sails are set opposite to the other half... so that during violent storms, half will be carried to shore to provide food for beach creatures while the other half will survive to continue drifting.

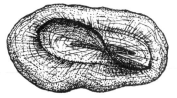

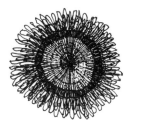

While drifting out at sea, the by-the-wind-sailor's tentacles provide a meal for a fragile **violet sea snail** (*Janthina janthina*) which lives nearby on a float made of bubbles. The snail's body is heavier than water so it needs the bubble raft to stay afloat. Its deep purple color comes from eating the by-the-wind-sailor.

When I see an out-of-place mound of bubbles rising from the wrack, I check it because it usually has a fragile purple snail attached to it, the maker of the bubbles.

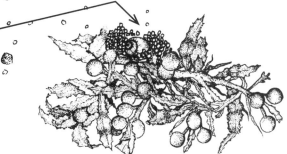

The violet sea snail also hangs around with **blue buttons jellyfish** (*Porpita porpita*) Like the by-the-wind-sailor, it floats on the ocean's surface, letting the Gulf Stream carry it to shore.

There is a nameless fascination about collecting... there is always something ahead to look to and strive for... There is something akin to the gloating feeling of a miser about it, even if the one getting the material together has no real scientific knowledge. But when one really gets interested in the living things, when one begins to study their relationships, past history and migrations, then one has something really worth while.

—Charles Torrey Simpson, *Florida Wild Life*

Worms or What?

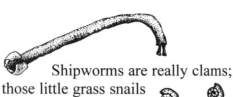

Shipworms are really clams; those little grass snails

worm shells are really snails; are really marine worms;

and worm rock is neither rock nor worm.

Shipworms (*Teredo navalis*) are really mollusks, little clam diggers who create holes and burrows in wood. The little quarter-inch shells, like clam shells, have razor-sharp edges that bite through wood, dragging behind a body that's way too big (6 to 12 inches) to fit in its little shell home. They enter the wood as tiny larvae which create the pinholes we see in driftwood. As the shipworm grows, the holes and burrows become wider and deeper.

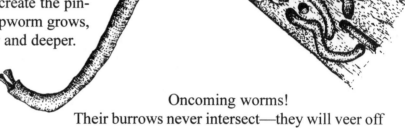

Oncoming worms! Their burrows never intersect—they will veer off to avoid another shipworm heading their way. This is what makes the interesting patterns in driftwood. Sometimes we can see the abandoned shell of a doomed shipworm left in the burrow.

Columbus was marooned in Jamaica for a year because two of his ships were ruined by shipworms during his fourth voyage.

Worm shells (*Vermicularia spirata* and *Vermicularia knorrii*) are small marine snails, not worms, even though they have a wormy shape. These are loners, but a related species will form colonies called worm rock that is sometimes mistaken for coral. ↙ ↘

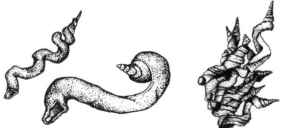

Worm rock ↗ (*Petaloconchus floridanus*) is composed of many mollusks living in colonies. Sometimes you see a single one, just a squiggle, attached to a shell or real rock.

Respect the common things. They are common because they survived.
—John C. Gifford, *Living by the Land*

Snails, Squirts and Stars

Those tiny (1/8-inch) snails that grow on turtle grass are **Spirorbis** (*Spirorbis spirillum*), hard-tube worms. They always coil clockwise. (A related species (*Spirorbis borealis*) coils counterclockwise. How come?) →

One of the tentacles on their head forms a plug when the animal is all the way inside. →

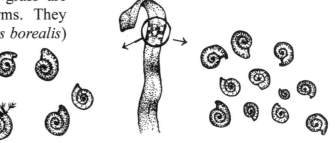

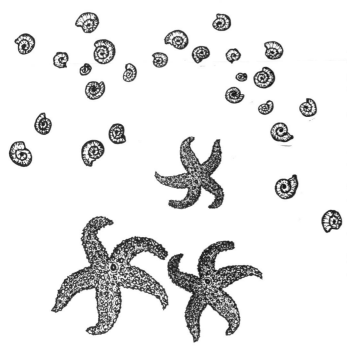

Every year for a week or two in the winter, **sea squirts** (*Styela plicata*) wash onto the lower beach. My friend Joan says they look like globs of pulsating raw beef liver.

Sea squirts are actually clusters of hundreds of tiny animals all bound together by an external covering like a tunic. (They're also known as "tunicates.")

You can touch sea squirts (no harm) to feel the richness of their slimy texture, but if you squeeze them, you'll find out why they're called sea squirts.   ↘

↑ **Sea stars** (*Echinoderma*, "spiny-skinned") are tossed onto our beaches from rough tides which they can't survive. In their own environment out at sea, they are strong, agile and aggressive. They use suckers (under their arm tips) to grip shells and pry them open. They then turn their stomachs inside out to surround the shell and digest the meat. It digests the animal there. Real fast food.

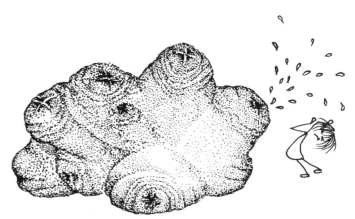

← When threatened, a sea star can drop off an arm, hoping its predator will be satisfied with that. It doesn't always work out that way, but when it does, the sea star can later grow its arm back. If a sea star is cut in two, it will become two sea stars. Scientists are using them for regeneration research.

Tests of Strength

If a sea star attacks a sea urchin, it will cram its stomach into the urchin's mouth and pull the urchin meat into its own body.

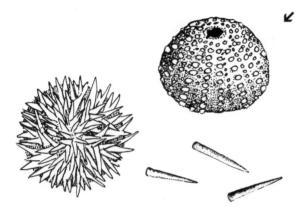

The empty shells of **sea urchins** are called "tests." When the urchin dies, the spines are no longer connected to the body by the outer muscle layer.

Sea urchin gonads are a delicacy in sushi.

Euell Gibbons in *Stalking the Faraway Places* writes that the urchin's roe rivals the best caviar in the world. The cooked roe tastes like scrambled eggs. He also writes that sea urchin roe can be substituted for oysters in oyster stew.

Sand dollars are related to sea urchins but have shortened spines. We find the tests (the hard inside skeletons) on the beach, or at least pieces of them mixed in with the wrack. The tiny five holes in the middle of the test are intake valves used to draw in water which operate their tube feet by hydraulic pressure.

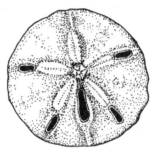

Sea cucumbers, even though they don't seem very sophisticated, are the most evolved of the **echinoderms** (sea stars and urchins). They are the first of their group to develop a *front* and a *back* even though they are apparently confused about which end does what: Sometimes they eat from the same end they use to poop. The anus is a richly endowed organ: the **five-toothed cucumber** has five shiny white teeth in its behind and a little fish called the pearlfish lives inside. Why?

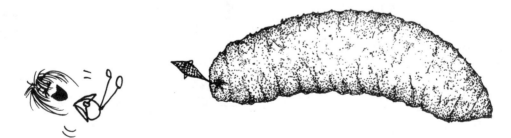

Sea cucumbers have no arms to sacrifice when threatened, but they will spew out their innards and later regenerate new innards.

Sea Cucumbers are also edible: "Split them open, gut them, dry them in the sun; then smoke them for twenty hours. They resemble burnt sausages by this time, but the Chinese ask for nothing better as hors d'oeuvres."

—Lawrence G. Green, *South African Beachcomber*

Some Birds

Herring gulls, ring-billed gulls, laughing gulls, willets, dowitchers, plovers, red knots, ruddy turn-stones, dunlins and sanderlings hang around Florida's barrier islands looking for food and water. Some of them need to rest during their long migrations south in the fall and north in the spring. Sometimes they decide to stay in Florida.

Migrating birds use favorite stopovers from year to year during their long flights, looking for seasonal berries, flowers and trees. Where do they go when their familiar resting spots have been replaced by shopping centers and office buildings?

Land to Sea... or... Sea to Land?

Ghost crabs (*Ocypode quadrata*) are the cleaning crew of the beaches, picking up and eating the rotting fish, seaweed debris and marine particles.

Like no other shore creatures, ghost crabs use the entire beach as their territory, tip-clawing from the surf to the dunes to undersand burrows. The burrows tunnel off at 45 degrees, then angle back and forth until they go back out through the sand again as an emergency escape hole.

Ghost crabs are mostly night creatures, foraging through beach debris for bits of rotting mollusk meat or discarded fish carcasses.

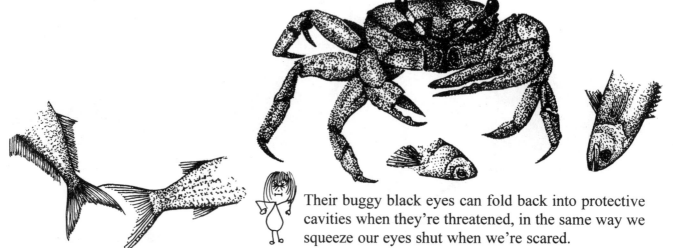

Their buggy black eyes can fold back into protective cavities when they're threatened, in the same way we squeeze our eyes shut when we're scared.

Ghost crabs give us a glimpse into the evolutionary process—they are evolving from sea to land creatures! They started life in the ocean, but at this point of their evolution, they're losing their ability to swim. They avoid the ocean, but still breathe through gills that need to be kept moist with sea water.

We see the reverse in evolution too—land animals that have gone to the sea: **sea turtles**. Compare the egg laying habits: sea turtles come from the sea to lay eggs on land; ghost crabs leave the land to lay eggs at sea. Do they both still have "memories" from millions of years ago?

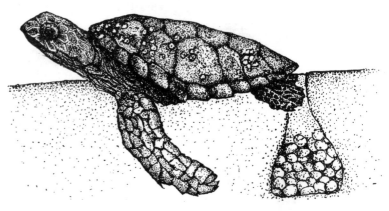

In 1969, a shrimper from North Carolina saw hundreds of **loggerheads** (*Caretta caretta*) clustering around the muddy water by Port Canaveral. Dredging around the Navy's Trident submarine basin had stirred up magnetic particles which attracted the sea turtles. This led researchers to discover that these sea turtles have ferromagnetic crystals in their brains that work as compasses. These crystals are found in other migratory creatures such as homing pigeons, porpoises and yellowfin tuna. Swimming just inside the Gulf Stream, sea turtles navigate within magnetic corridors, using these internal compasses as guides.

Sea Turtles

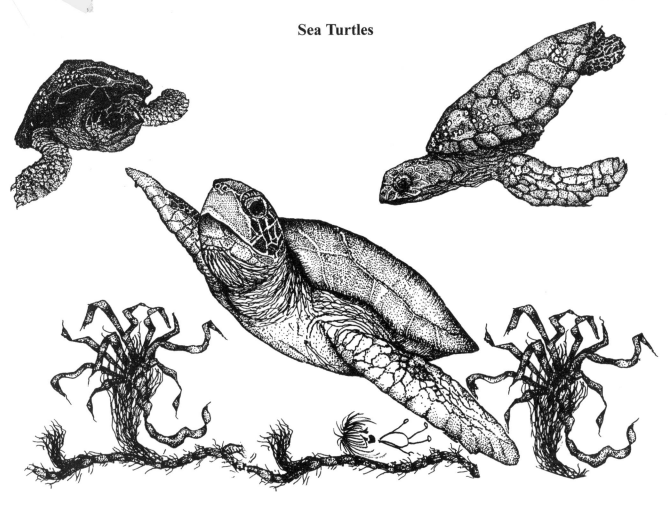

Although we typically associate sea turtles with the ocean since we see them laying eggs on our beach in the summer, younger sea turtles use our estuaries as a "developmental habitat." Juvenile **green sea turtles** (*Chelonia mydas*) and loggerheads use some estuaries for nourishment, shelter, and learning skills while maturing. Once they're mature enough to exist in the ocean, they probably won't return to their growing-up river.

According to documents written in the 1800s, sea turtles used to be so plentiful in the Indian River Lagoon in Brevard County that they provided a lucrative "turtle fishery" industry. Green turtles were the primary target of the fishery because their tasty meat had a high market value. Loggerhead meat, on the other hand, was tough, strong, and musky, but loggerheads were caught in the nets unintentionally. Since they were considered a nuisance by-catch (as were sharks, stingrays, and sawfish), they were routinely slaughtered.

By 1878, the commercial turtle fisheries had become so productive that in one year, eight fishermen captured 1600 green turtles. In 1896, a Sebastian fisherman took 2500 turtles from the Indian River Lagoon.

During this same era, thousands of sea turtle eggs were taken from the beach, and female turtles were turned over on their backs for a sport called "turtle turning." These activities obviously contributed to the decline in sea turtle numbers. Nowadays, we don't see thousands of turtles in the Indian River Lagoon as described in these early reports, but both green and loggerhead turtles still use the Lagoon system as a "growing up" area.

At Loggerheads

If you haven't yet witnessed a 200-pound loggerhead sea turtle crawling from the sea to lay her eggs, you're in for a night of natural beauty that no video can capture. Through the summer on Central Florida's barrier islands—the largest loggerhead nesting area in the western hemisphere—you can see these ancient sea creatures come out of the ocean to crawl onto the beach just as they did 200 million years ago.

Late at night during the summer, each female loggerhead returns to her own birth spot to dig a hole and lay 100 to 150 eggs. The eggs look like a pile of ping pong balls deep within the hole. She keeps plopping them out until she's finished. Then she twists and turns until the hole is covered with sand. The eggs don't break because they're leathery and flexible.

The eggs incubate for about 2 months in the warm summer sun. The temperature of the sand during incubation determines the hatchlings' sex.

From the moment they emerge from the sand, always as a group, tiny loggerhead hatchlings struggle to stay alive—they dehydrate if they don't reach the ocean soon after surfacing, then ghost crabs, raccoons, birds and later sharks all go after the 2-inch creatures for food.

Unless bright lights distract them, the hatchlings can navigate with remarkable accuracy. Not only do they use the Earth's magnetic field to navigate, they somehow know to swim into the waves. During Hurricane Hugo in 1989 when wave directions were reversed, hatchlings would swim back to shore because they kept wanting to swim into the waves.

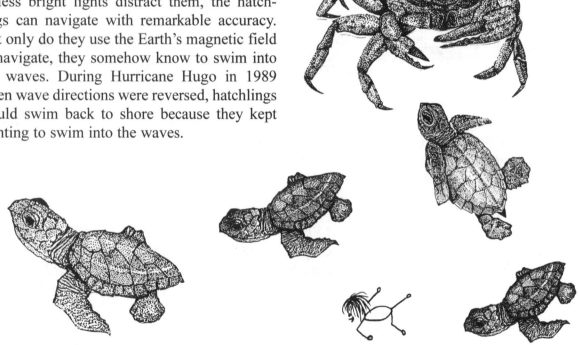

The migratory paths of young Florida loggerheads follow the same clockwise direction of the Sargasso Sea. As a matter of fact, sea turtles swim around the Sargasso Sea many times before returning to their birth area years later. In deeper water, where wave action isn't defined, they resort to using the magnetic field. They also use a "mapping" sense to locate the exact spot of their home area. These extraordinary navigation abilities have made them an evolutionary success, enabling them to use feeding grounds far away from their nesting areas. Their near extinction is a result of decades of slaughter for their meat.

More Sea Turtles

Hatchlings shouldn't be picked up by humans, even to help them get to the water; they need to "map" their path, like programming a computer. Otherwise they have no internal instructions to guide them back to their natal area years later.

Although not as common as the loggerhead on Florida's beaches, other sea turtles arrive in the summer to lay their eggs. Here you can see the different sizes of their carapaces.

Loggerhead

Leatherback   Green   Hawksbill   Kemp's Ridley

Sea turtles eat dangerous box jellyfish, Portuguese men-of-war and glass sponges which would kill any other mammal. Do the turtles have a protective lining that keeps them from being poisoned? Even though sea turtles are immune to the jellyfish's stings, they apparently get a narcotic high from eating them; their eyes become puffy and red, and in the midst of a feeding frenzy, they lose their normally superb coordination.

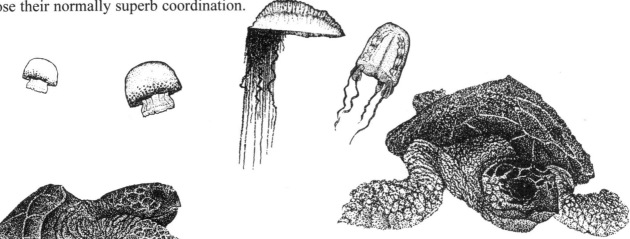

Sea turtles for the most part are solitary animals. No parental care is given to eggs or hatchlings and contact between adults is limited to courtship... Hatchlings, however, must work together to escape from the nest and cross the beach and turtles of all species may be found in large groups of their own kind feeding or traveling. Except during courtship and mating there appears to be little interaction between individuals in a group.

—From *Florida's Sea Turtles*, by Florida Power & Light Company

THE SHORE

When we go down to the low-tide line, we enter a world that is as old as the earth itself—the primeval meeting place of the elements of earth and water, a place of compromise and conflict and eternal change.

—Rachel Carson, *The Edge of the Sea*

A Little History

The shore between Cape Canaveral and Melbourne Beach was used by the Ais Indians more than 7000 years ago. Shell mounds called *middens* were dumping grounds for shells and bones, and many of them still remain. One of the middens in Cape Canaveral was so high it could be seen from offshore and was used by early sailors as a landmark.

Just imagine the Ais fishing from the same shore as today's anglers. Canaveral National Seashore, a 24-mile strip of undeveloped beach, is how all of Florida's coast used to look with more than 300 species of birds and 700 species of plants. Less than one mile south, you can see the launch gantries used by NASA and the military to launch missiles and rockets into space.

Artificial reefs about 20 miles east of Port Canaveral were created by blowing up old Air Force fuel tanks. Known as the *Titan-US Air Force Reef*, 230 tons of steel were dropped 120 feet to the bottom. Dozens of other official and unofficial reefs exist, made from old launch pads, buses, washing machines, cars and concrete waste. These reefs provide excellent surfing and windsurfing conditions.

Natural reefs off Central Florida's coast are made of long strips of coquina and wormrock. The offshore water is too cold for the elaborate coral reefs that thrive in South Florida. Coquina reefs and the artificial reefs provide shelter and feeding areas for small marine animals, turtles and lots of fish—a good environment for surf fishing.

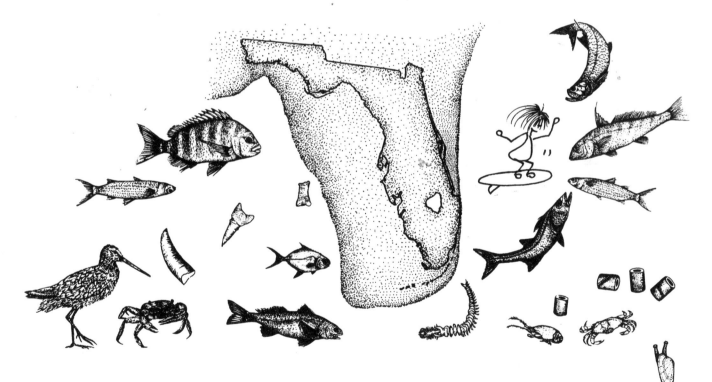

The shore is the seam of the coast, connecting land with sea; the transition zone where special land-sea creatures are the threads that hold the seam together. The Gulf Stream, "a river in the ocean," carries nutrients and warmth to shore creatures like coquinas, mole crabs, parchment worms and shore birds.

Muddy Waters

Thousands of the little pastel **coquinas** (*Donax variabilis*) work their way with the tides, and travel up and down the shore with the seasons, constantly catching food particles. As the tide moves in every 12 hours and 25 minutes, so does the coquina, always looking for food.

Much of the sand on the beach is made up of tiny pieces of coquina shell.

In the same wet area where coquinas search for food, **mole crabs** (*Emerita talpoida*), also migrate with the tides, catching food particles with their feathery antennas. They do everything backward: swim, dig, crawl and eat. These one-inch land-sea creatures always face the ocean.

When mole crabs burrow backward into the wet sand, the branches of the two antennae press together to form a breathing tube, which is what we see sticking out from the sand.

Only half the size of the females, the males are completely dependent on them. In the winter when the female moves into deeper water, the males (sometimes two or three) cling to her back, getting a free ride and free food along the way.

The female also carries her clusters of eggs for several months, until she releases the larvae into the ocean to mature. By the time the tiny mole crabs become *megalops* ("giant eyes"), they're ready to return from the water to begin life in the wet sand.

During storms, thousands of mole crabs wash up onto higher beaches where they can't survive because they need the constant flow of water. But, in turn, they become food for fish, birds and ghost crabs. Even their empty shells are used by scavenger insects as protection from heat.

I think my ancestors were from the shore. I don't mean my great grandparents who lived near the North Sea; I mean some land-sea creatures who lived in the shore millions of years ago. My directional dysfunction and morning inertia disappear when I'm in the surf—I have a sense of fitting and contentment that I have nowhere else. Maybe I was a ghost crab millions of years ago—like me, they come alive on the beach at night.

Who Knew?

Those papery tubes that we find on the beach at the end of each summer are the discarded houses of **parchment worms** (*Chaetopterus pergamentaceus*). Who ever would have thought that those beautiful creatures lived in those wrinkled old tubes?

Parchment worms, about 5 inches long, live in U-shaped tubes, each end sticking out of the wet sand like little chimneys. Water is sucked in from one end of the tube for oxygen and food particles, while the other end discharges waste. The middle section of the worm's intricate body has three paddles used to pump water through the tube.

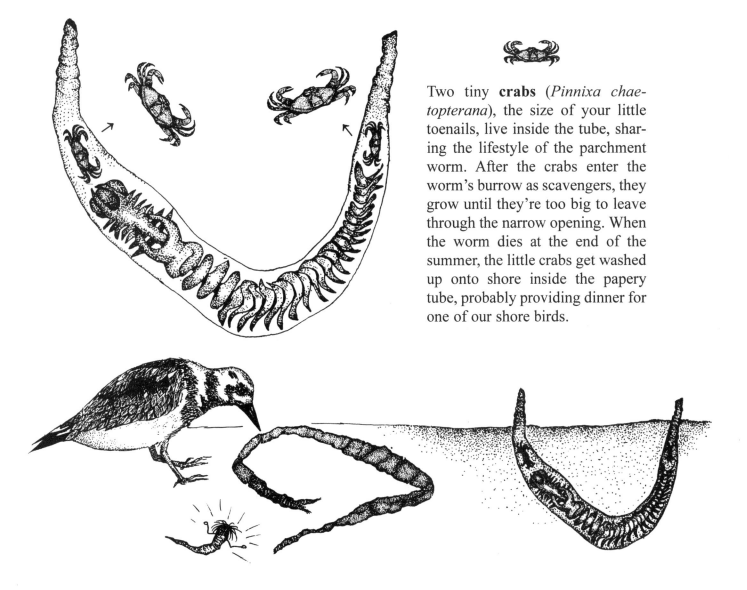

Two tiny **crabs** (*Pinnixa chaetopterana*), the size of your little toenails, live inside the tube, sharing the lifestyle of the parchment worm. After the crabs enter the worm's burrow as scavengers, they grow until they're too big to leave through the narrow opening. When the worm dies at the end of the summer, the little crabs get washed up onto shore inside the papery tube, probably providing dinner for one of our shore birds.

If you carried a live parchment worm home and put it in a pitch-black room, you'd see it glow with a magnificent blue light. Why would a worm that spends its entire life buried in a tube underground need to light up?

In minimus Natura praestat ("Nature excels in the least things").

—Pliny the Elder (Roman naturalist 23–79 A.D.)

Shore Birds

Gulls change their feather colors (plumage) from season to season: they also change from year to year, between sexes, and as they go through courting and mating. I've given up trying to figure out gull colors. I know all young gulls are brown (sort of) and that's enough.

They need their space.

Gulls communicate by prancing, puffing and ducking, signals that other gulls know how to interpret. Some gulls won't tolerate another bird standing less than a foot away; they're very specific about the distance, even one inch over is too much. The offender is warned by hostile expressions to back off; if the warning is ignored, drastic action is in order:

The Herring Gull that spies an unwelcome visitor on his turf adopts his most threatening posture and stance and slowly walks toward the other bird. When the trespasser refuses to budge, the owner bends down and rips out a large mouthful of grass, a challenge that the other bird may accept by doing the same. The birds may then sit opposite each other and attempt to pull the grass from each other's beaks. The battle can escalate until wings are beating against wings, beaks furiously pecking one another.

—Lester L. Short, *The Lives of Birds*

Gull Migration: Is it genetic?

Why don't all gulls migrate? To determine if a gull is born with an internal code to migrate, a test was done interchanging eggs between non-migrating herring gulls and migrating lesser black-billed gulls. Nine hundred chicks were reared by foster parents of the opposite species. The young birds were banded and later recovered. So what happened? Many of the non-migrating gulls raised by migrating foster parents followed their foster parents, and the migratory nestlings reared by stay-at-home foster parents also migrated. Go figure.

↗ **Laughing gulls** (*Larus atricilla*) look like they just stuck their heads in a bucket of black paint.

The **ring-billed gull** (*Larus delawarensis*) is one of the smallest of the gulls and one of the most common to Florida's shore.

44

More Shore Birds

Dowitchers, red knots, dunlins, willets, ibis, pelicans, and great blue herons are some of the most beautiful birds in the world. We can see them any time we want. Now, anyway.

← **Dowitchers** (*Limnodromus griseus*) are pale in winter and darker brown in summer. They are usually only in Florida in the winter.

Red knots (*Calidris canutus*) nest and raise their young in the Arctic, but they stop in Florida during their migration to South America in the fall. Some of them stay with us through the year. We see them poking their short bills in the sand trying to find coquinas.

Dunlins (*Calidris alpina*) follow the breaking surf, back and forth, back and forth. Their thick bills are slightly curved down, and in the spring, their plain coloring changes to bright rust and black.

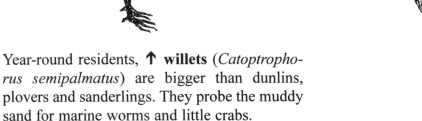

Year-round residents, ↑ **willets** (*Catoptrophorus semipalmatus*) are bigger than dunlins, plovers and sanderlings. They probe the muddy sand for marine worms and little crabs.

Skittish and energetic, **sanderlings** (*Calidris alba*) are the most common of the sandpipers and we see them in flocks all year, dodging the surf as they look for little marine creatures.

45

More Shore Birds

Moving up and down with the tides, looking for crabs and shellfish, is the **ibis** (*Eudocimus albus*), about two feet high with bright orange legs and bill. In flight, their stark white bodies contrast with their black-tipped wings. They soar in arcs, looking for unoccupied areas of beach to rest and feed. They land together and move up the beach in unison.

Poking their curved bills in and out of the sand like efficient sewing machines, ibis pull out mole crabs and other little marine creatures. Among the flock, a few brown immature ibis are usually seen, staying close to the adults.

Ploffskin, Pluffskin, Pelican jee!
We think no bird's so happy as we!
Plumpskin, Ploshkin, Pelican jill!
We think so then, and we thought so still!

—Edward Lear, *Complete Nonsense Book*

In the '60s, the **brown pelican** (*Pelecanus occidentalis*) in Florida was almost extinct because of DDT poisoning, but outlawing DDT helped them to make a good comeback. In Louisiana, they disappeared completely until Florida created a program to help them "re-stock" their pelican population.

For all their bulky clumsiness on land, brown pelicans are graceful flyers, using air currents to maneuver and glide effortlessly over the ocean. They fly in formation, the strongest usually leading and setting the pace.

But the pelicans are best seen as they fly in an orderly line from somewhere shoreward, out to the ship inspection. Several flocks of ten or a dozen came alternately flapping and sailing, their wings all beating time with those of the leader as if in a careful drill movement. They sailed over the ship and then settled upon the water, still in an orderly row, and I thought I saw each flock confer after sitting and wag bald heads and long beards as if in approval.

—Winthrop Packard, *Florida Trails*

...And More Shore Birds

Seasonal changes in pelicans' plumage colors are the most elaborate of just about any bird; during courtship, their heads are an intense yellow. From then on, the neck, eyes bill, and pouch change to various combinations of yellows, pinks, browns and oranges.

A Family Affair

In January, both males and females have yellow heads to attract each other during courting. Mating is a ritualized and intricate performance, done in the nearby mangroves. The male picks out a nesting site and tries to attract a female by moving his head sideways in a figure eight. If he's too aggressive, he scares her away, but if he's too subtle, she won't notice. He continues until a female notices his erotic display and approaches him. Once she steps into his area, a match is made.

Pelicans are silent. Only the very young make a hoarse croak, asking for food. To eat, the young plunge their beaks down into the parents' gullets where processed food is available.

If the young pelicans are threatened, the adults will heave a mess of stinky fish at the offender.

At about 11 weeks, the young are ready to leave the nest to begin training. Young pelicans train with their parents in calm waters, imitating shallow dives until they're strong and agile enough to dive from heights of 30 to 40 feet. I've watched young pelicans practice for hours—circle, dive, rest—circle, dive, rest—over and over until they have enough confidence to try a trickier maneuver.

Pelicans' incredible underwater abilities suggest that they are descended from a fish-bird (*Ichthyornis*) from more than 30 million years ago.

Fishing

Late every night I see a **great blue heron** (*Ardea herodias*) in the shallow water by Melbourne Beach Pier. I've watched her pull snakes from the muddy sand and plunge her sharp bill through the water to come up with squirmy fish. After watching her night after night for more than a year, I noticed she was gone for one or two nights each week; then it occurred to me that it was always on Saturday and Sunday. How did she know she could take the weekends off? I was slow to realize that I saw her on those days at the beach when weekend anglers were contributing part of their catch to her. After those free meals, she was probably too full to bother with her night river fishing.

Long legs and wide-spread toes make it easy for great blue herons to patrol muddy waters.

When I see a **mullet** (*Mugil cephalus*) bursting from the water's surface like a Trident missile, I know something big must be chasing it.

I found nature full of unexpected kindnesses, mercies, and joy. I learned to live intimately with nature in a spirit of cooperation and love, bolstered by deep respect for her ways.

—Euell Gibbons, *Beachcomber's Handbook*

Fishing

When an angler hooks a **tarpon** (*Megalops atlanticus*) you hear it:

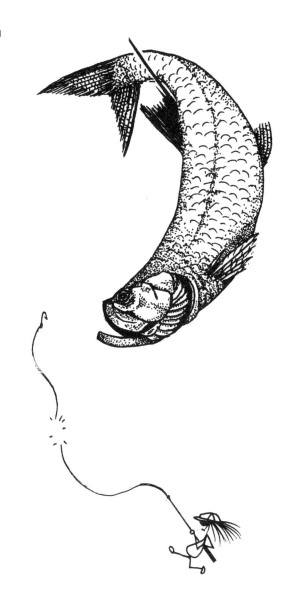

"...the fish goes up in a twisting, head-shaking, gill rattling explosion of saltwater, towering up there against the noonday sun, higher than your head, painting herself forever against that tropic sky, and then she falls back with a crash like a locomotive going off at the end of the dock..."

(Frank Sargeant, *The Tarpon Book*)*

Tarpon will eat just about anything, dead or alive. They come in close enough to shore to cast right to them, especially in clear, gentle surf when the mullet are running.

Spawning occurs in the open sea; up to 19 million *leptocephalus* ("skinny no-head-larvae") born in the sea fight their way back to their ancestral homes along the shore. The few that survive keep going inland, hiding in sea grass and mangrove roots in inch-deep water—they can take in air from the surface.

When they're two or three years old, they begin to move back out to sea.

It takes 50 years for a tarpon to grow to 150 pounds. It takes less than one hour to kill it.

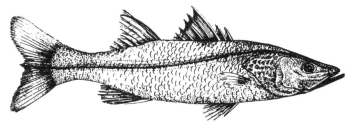

Beautiful silvery fish with a distinct black lateral line, **snook** ↖ (*Centropomis undecimalis*) comb the surf day and night from spring through the fall looking for food. They actively feed in rising water since the rise brings mole crabs and sand fleas out of their holes, and small fish close to shore.

Snook can't be caught much farther north than Cape Canaveral, unless the temperatures become warmer than usual. Temperatures below 60°F will kill them.

Peak spawning occurs in the summer; tides carry hundreds of thousands of eggs into estuaries where they begin life one or two days after the eggs are released. After one year, they're about 7 inches, after two years they're about 14 inches, but after three years growth slows. Age is determined by *otoliths*, (ear bones) which show annual rings, like trees. Since all large snook are females (males rarely are found over 10 years old), they may undergo a sex change as they age, like groupers.

*Fishing is one of the most literary of all sports: angling literature started with *Treatyse of Fysshinge With an Angle*, printed in 1496 by Wynkyn do Worde. In 1653 Izaak Walton's *Compleat Angler* was published; it has since gone through more than 300 printings.

Fishing

← **Redfish** (*Sciaenops ocellatus*) almost disappeared in the '80s, but fish conservation efforts paid off and they've made a good comeback. Responsible anglers still release undersize redfish with care, knowing how vulnerable these fish are to overkill. Their longevity is about 20 years.

Whiting (*Menticirrhus americanus*) will eat just about anything; clams, cut mullet, sand fleas. Because they are a bottom fish, they can live on small shellfish.

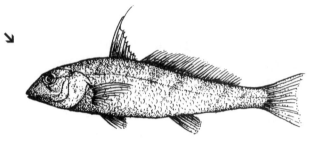

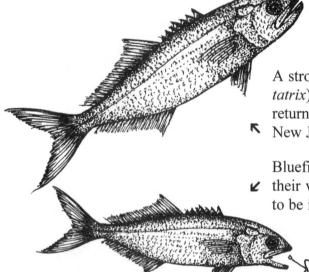

A strong migration of northeast **bluefish** (*Pomatomus saltatrix*) to Florida's coast occurs in the winter. Some of them return, but lots of the big ones just don't want to go back to New Jersey.

Bluefish are the most bloodthirsty of ocean fish and will eat their way through a school of small fish; if bathers happen to be in their path, the blues will tear up their legs.

Sheepshead (*Archosargus probatocephalus*) feed on mollusks like clams and barnacles: look at those teeth… they were made for scraping barnacles off pilings. Their teeth give them their sheep-like appearance and name.

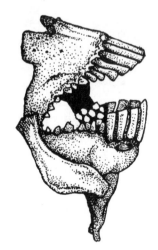

↖ Sheepshead move in and out with the tides, following the crustaceans' migrations.

Fishing and Beyond

The ocean tides influence the movements of **pompano** (*Trachinotus carolinus*). When mole crabs and mollusks come out to feed in shallow water, pompano will swim close to shore in 3-inch water.

Looking toward the horizon, we can see **Atlantic bottlenosed dolphin** (*Tursiops truncatus*) swimming, playing and training their young. I love watching the adults flip their young in the air.

Dolphins follow trawlers to feed on discarded seafood. They use echo-location to listen to the echo of their own sound beams to help locate objects.

Between December and March, **right whales** (*Eubalaena glacialis*) end their migration offshore around Central Florida's coast; this is their calving area, so it's possible to see adults with young whales nearby.

These whales were named *right whales* in the 1800s because the value of their oil and meat was so "right" that they were almost marketed out of existence. Today, only a few hundred still exist in the world.

The lesson clearly is that we should stick to the time-tested things. Things that are here, are here because they are fit.

—John C. Gifford, *Living by the Land*

THE DUNES

We boast of our civilization, our Christianity, our wonderful knowledge and accomplishments. We build and operate hospitals wherein we tenderly care for the sick, the deformed, the mentally deficient, we coddle the vilest criminals in our penitentiaries and jails but we have savagely and senselessly destroyed our wild life; we have swept from the earth what the poor, untaught Indian left intact... all the skill, all the science in the world cannot revive a dead animal, they cannot restore a single species of plant that has been exterminated.

—Charles Torrey Simpson, *Florida Wild Life*

A Little Geography

Three-hundred million years ago, Florida ripped away from Africa. Thirty million years ago, it rose out of the sea and gradually became a peninsula twice as wide as it is now. This wide peninsula still exists and is called the Florida Plateau. This undersea land is the continental shelf which extends away from the west coast about 100 miles. However, not much of the shelf extends from most of Florida's east coast, so it's more vulnerable to the full force of the ocean.

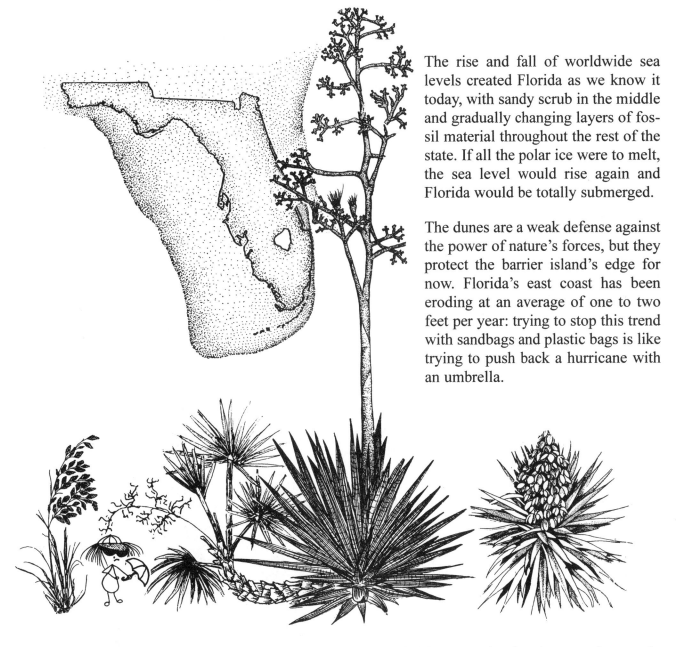

The rise and fall of worldwide sea levels created Florida as we know it today, with sandy scrub in the middle and gradually changing layers of fossil material throughout the rest of the state. If all the polar ice were to melt, the sea level would rise again and Florida would be totally submerged.

The dunes are a weak defense against the power of nature's forces, but they protect the barrier island's edge for now. Florida's east coast has been eroding at an average of one to two feet per year: trying to stop this trend with sandbags and plastic bags is like trying to push back a hurricane with an umbrella.

The combined roots of native dune plants form an invisible network of underground strength, weaving horizontally, vertically and diagonally to stabilize the mounds of sand that protect our coast against pounding tides. When the ocean's forces weaken the root structure, the dunes start to erode, but sometimes the strength of one last root will hold enough to rebuild an entire system.

Though I do not believe that a plant will spring up where no seed has been, I have great faith in a seed. Convince me that you have a seed there, and I am prepared to expect wonders.

—Henry David Thoreau

Dune Plants

Most plants can't survive in the dunes because of the nutrient-low soil with no decaying matter. But dune plants are able to compensate: Broad strong leaves to catch salt spray (sea grapes); hairy leaves to trap moisture (Indian blanket flower); flexible stems to withstand winds (sea oats); and twisting vines to cling to the sand (beach morning glory). All of them have far-reaching roots to absorb any available moisture.

Saw palmetto (*Serenoa repens*), a scrubby palm used as medicine for centuries is now used in treating prostate conditions. The therapeutic effect of the liposterolic (fat and sterol) extract of saw palmetto berries improves the symptoms of enlarged prostates. Its effectiveness is from its ability to inhibit a compound that causes the prostate cells to multiply excessively.

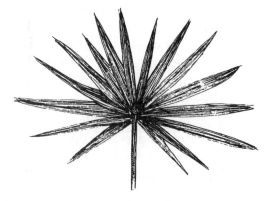

The bluish-black cherry-size fruit is eaten by raccoons and opossums. Native Americans ate them too, but Jonathan Dickinson, who was shipwrecked in the 1690s, said they tasted like "rotten cheese steeped in tobacco juice."

South Florida pioneers mixed palmetto berry juice with carbonated water and sold it as a soft drink called *Metto*.

Sea grapes (*Coccoloba uvifera*), dune plants nearest the ocean, shield those behind from winds and salt spray with their large tough leaves. It's a wonderful plant, not only because it's so attractive or because it can grow high, low or fill in patches between other dune plants, but also because you can eat it any time of the year right from the plant.

The berries ripen a few at a time; the best way to get the fruit is to shake the plant and let the ripe ones fall. The berries can be made into jelly and the juice can be used in baking muffins and cakes. Marian Van Atta, in *Living Off The Land*, includes some wonderful recipes using sea grapes.

Only female sea grape plants have fruit; the males show dead flower stalks. A resin from cuts in the bark ("kino") is a good source for astringent medications.

Dangerous Plants... Watch out!

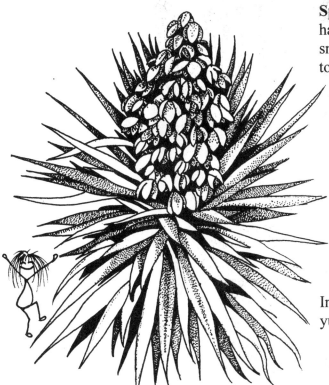

Spanish bayonet or **Yucca cactus** (*Yucca aloifolia*) has dagger-like leaves which gave it the nickname snooper plant. It used to be planted under windows to keep burglars and snoopers away.

Cream-colored flowers grow in clusters from the center during the summer; the flowers are edible, raw or cooked, and have a nice nutty flavor. Adding yucca flower petals will jazz up any old plain salad.

Almost all parts of this plant can be eaten. The fruit grows up to 5 inches with purple skin; lots of people bake it with butter and add sea purslane for seasoning.

In World War II, 80 million pounds of fiber from yucca leaves were used to make burlap bags.

I've seen a field of **nickernut** shrubs (*Caesalpinia bonduc*) growing in the dunes at Port Canaveral. Their prickly pods turn brown at the end of summer and when the pods are dry enough, they crack open and seeds as hard as marbles pop out, roll down the inlet bank and drift out to sea. Hundreds of them float through the inlet, drifting for years in the ocean's currents until they wash up on another beach somewhere else in the world.

These pretty seeds are called sea pearls because they're smooth, shiny and round, so who would think that this gem-like seed could come from a nasty and painful shrub? I grew one from seed and within a year it was taller than my house. Every time I walked by, it reached out to scratch me with its razor sharp tiny spikes. It was the meanest plant I ever had, but it kept burglars away. When it grows on the dunes, it keeps humans from trampling on the other dune plants.

The gray seeds are poisonous but the bark has been used as a quinine substitute ("poor man's quinine") to treat malaria. Young leaves were used at one time for toothaches and the oil in the seeds were used to treat arthritis.

Dune Plants

Another painful but beautiful dune resident is the **prickly pear** (*Opuntia humifusa*). It can grow up to 6 feet, but typically we see them growing to about 2 feet. The pads are covered with clusters of fine sharp spikes. Showy flowers, usually yellow, blossom through the spring into the fall, followed by red plump fruit.

The fruit juice can be mixed with other juices or used in baking breads and cakes. The cactus pads can be cut up and cooked like green beans. Marian Van Atta explains how to remove the spikes and gives more recipes in her book *Living Off The Land*.

Almost all parts of this cactus have been used medicinally for ailments including pleurisy, ulcers, tumors, diarrhea, asthma and a long list of others.

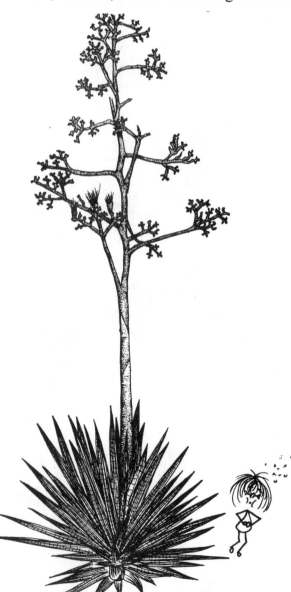

A **century plant** (*Agave*) will reach maturity in 10 to 50 years (not 100 years as its name implies) when a thick stem shoots up from the middle of the plant. When the stalk begins to grow, it can shoot up 2 inches per day until it's taller than a telephone pole and thicker than a baby's thigh.

After blooming, the plant dies but *bulbils,* which grow at the stem top, fall and grow new plants.

Century plants help stabilize soil on dry sloping dunes and their roots form a dense mat just below the surface so they can absorb even the slightest rain.

A century plant provides food all year. The starchy heart, as big as a cabbage, has a hot flavor, and the young flower stalk is a tasty vegetable. The flowers can be eaten raw, and fresh juice comes from the flower stalk, called *aqua miel*—when distilled it's called *mescal* (Mexicans called it *tequila*—"to-kill-ya").

Dune Plants

Beach sunflower (*Helianthus debilis*), a low-growing plant, is in bloom all year. Look closely and once in awhile you'll see a small bee with bright yellow wings matching the flower petals in color and shape.

Sandburs (*Cenchrus spinifex*) are good for stopping dune-damaging foot traffic. Their smaller roots contribute to the intricate root network stabilizing the sand.

↗ **Sea oats** (*Uniola paniculata*) are the tallest and most common of the grassy dune plants. Because they are critical to the dune plant system, Florida state law prohibits endangering them in any way. Their root system is a strong far-reaching mass of tangled stems and threads that stabilize the sandy dune soil.

A weed is just a plant out of place.
—John C. Gifford, *Reclamation of the Everglades With Trees*

Dune Plants

The beautiful yellow and orange petals of the **Indian blanket flower** (*Gaillardia pulchella*) are so common on Florida's dunes that I have a tendency to take them for granted.

The **coral bean** plant (*Erythrina herbacea*) has a wonderful character: long slender bright red jaunty flowers which attract hummingbirds during their spring and fall migrations; then its pods turn into lumpy strings of beads that dangle between the leaves.

The stems, leaves and seeds contain toxins but some substances are used medicinally as a muscle relaxant.

Sea purslane (*Sesuvium portulacastrum*) is a creeping plant with fleshy leaves and deep pink flowers. You can eat the leaves and stems raw or uncooked, but they're pretty salty uncooked. Rich in vitamins A and C, they are cultivated as a vegetable in Eastern Asia. I love eating scrambled eggs with chopped and cooked sea purslane.

The extinction of a rare plant or animal is a worldwide calamity.

—John C. Gifford, *Living by the Land*

Dune Plants

The **bay bean** (*Canavalia rosea*) is a sturdy, far-reaching vine with a strong root system that binds the edges of the dunes. The wide flat leaves are able to fold onto themselves during the hottest part of the day to reduce the heat-absorbing area.

The pods produce sea beans which I find near the dunes throughout the year.

Young bay bean pods are tender and can be eaten in salads or cooked like Chinese pea pods.

Beach morning glory (*Ipomoea pes-caprae*) is a hardy creeping vine like the bay bean, but this one stretches far down onto the beach away from the dunes. It is one of the two most important dune vines because it extends its tong trailing stems perpendicular to the dunes, daring to grow where no other plants will go. It can tolerate the intense heat from the beach sand, stabilizing the fragile lower area of the dunes

A tea can be made from the leaves and is used as a diuretic.

I think Evolution, so far as man was concerned, was a great mistake. It would have been better had there been only plants, and a few botanists to enjoy them.
—Professor Karl von Goebel in a letter to David Fairchild, *The World Grows Round My Door*

Bibliography

Abbott, Tucker R. *Collectible Florida Shells*. Melbourne, Florida: American Malacologists, Inc., 1984.

Amos, William A. *The Life of the Seashore*. New York: McGraw-Hill Book Co., 1966.

Berrill, N.J. *The Life of the Ocean*. New York: McGraw-Hill Book Co., 1966.

Brown, Robin, C. *Florida's Fossils*. Sarasota, Florida: Pineapple Press, 1988.

Carson, Rachel. *The Edge of the Sea*. Boston: Houghton Mifflin Co., 1956.

Donoghue, Michael and Ann Wheeler. *Save the Dolphins*. New York: Sheridan House, Inc., 1990.

Daniel, Thase. *Wings on the Southwind*. Birmingham, Alabama: Oxmoor House, Inc., 1984.

Fairchild, David. *The World Was My Garden: Travels of a Plant Explorer*. New York: Charles Scribner's Sons, 1938.

Florida Department of Environmental Protection, *Fishing Lines, Angler's Guide to Florida Marine Resources*.

Foster, Steven and James A. Duke. *Eastern/Central Medicinal Plants* (The Peterson Field Guide Series). Boston: Houghton Mifflin Co., 1990.

Gibbons, Euell. *Stalking the Blue-eyed Scallop*. Vermont: Alan C. Hood, 1964.

Gibbons, Euell. *Beachcomber's Handbook*. New York: David McKay Co., Inc., 1967.

Gifford, John C. *On Preserving Tropical Florida*. Coral Gables, Florida: University of Miami Press, 1972.

Gill, Joan E. and Beth R. Read. *Born of the Sun*. Hollywood, Florida: Florida Bicentennial Commemorative Journal, Inc., (Worth International Comm. Corp.), 1975.

Gosner, Kenneth L. *A Field Guide to the Atlantic Seashore*. Boston: Houghton Mifflin Co., 1978.

Green, Lawrence G. *South African Beachcomber*. Cape Town, South Africa: Howard Timmins, 1958.

Gunn, C. R. and J. V. Dennis. *World Guide to Tropical Drift Seeds and Fruits*. New York: Quadrangle/The New York Times Book Co., 1976.

Hargreaves, Dorothy and Bob Hargreaves. *Tropical Trees Found in the Caribbean, South America, Central America, Florida, Mexico*. Lahaina, Hawaii: Ross-Hargreaves (Division of L & M Equipment Co.), 1965.

Bibliography (continued)

Harris, Cricket. *Dictionary of Seashore Life*. St. Petersburg, Florida: Great Outdoors Publishing Co., 1961.

Kale, Herb and David Maehr. *Florida's Birds*. Sarasota, Florida: Pineapple Press, 1990.

Kaplan, Eugene H. *Southeastern and Caribbean Seashores* (Peterson Field Guide). Boston: Houghton Mifflin Co., 1988.

Kellersberger, Julia Lake. *Rooted in Florida Soil*. Melbourne, Florida: FIT Press, 1971.

Leip, Hans. *River in the Sea, The Story of the Gulf Stream*. New York: Putnam, 1957.

Lindbergh, Anne M. *Gift From the Sea*. New York: Vintage Books, 1991.

Mace, Alice E. *The Birds Around Us*. California: Ortho Books, 1986.

McKay, Frances P. *Let's Go Shelling*. St. Petersburg, Florida: Great Outdoors Publishing Co., 1968.

Meinkoth, Norman A. *The Audubon Society Field Guide to North American Seashore Creatures*. New York: Alfred A. Knopf, 1981.

Morris, Percy A. *Shells of the Atlantic* (Peterson Field Guide). Boston: Houghton Mifflin Co., 1975.

Morton, Julia. *Wild Plants for Survival in South Florida*. Miami, Florida: Fairchild Tropical Garden, 1990.

Nellis, David W. *Seashore Plants of South Florida and the Caribbean*. Florida: Pineapple Press, 1994.

Niering, William A. *The Audubon Society Field Guide to North American Wildflowers: Eastern Region*. New York: Alfred Knopf, 1979.

Page, Jake and Eugene S. Morton. *The Smithsonian Book of Birds, Lords of the Air*. New York: Orion Books, 1989.

Perrins, Christopher and C. J. O. Harrison. *Birds: Their Life, Their Ways, Their World*. New York: Reader's Digest Association, Inc., 1976.

Perry, Richard. *The Unknown Ocean* (Vol. I of *The Many Worlds of Wildlife Series*). New York: Taplinger Publishing Co., 1972.

Perry, Richard. *Life at the Sea's Frontiers* (Vol. III of *The Many Worlds of Wildlife Series*). New York: Taplinger Publishing Co., 1974.

Rudloe, Jack. *The Erotic Ocean*. New York: E. P. Dutton, Inc., 1984.

Bibliography (continued)

Rudloe, Jack. *Search for the Great Turtle Mother.* Sarasota, Florida: Pineapple Press, 1995.

Rudloe, Jack. *The Sea Brings Forth.* New York: Alfred A. Knopf, 1968.

Sanger, Marjory Bartlett. *World of the Great White Heron.* Toronto: Devin-Adair Co., 1967.

Sargent, Frank. *The Tarpon Book.* Florida: Larsen's Outdoor Publishing, 1991.

Sargent, Frank. *The Redfish Book.* Florida: Larsen's Outdoor Publishing, 1991.

Simpson, Charles Torrey. *Florida Wildlife.* New York: The MacMillan Co., 1932.

Short, Lester L. *The Lives of Birds: Birds of the World and Their Behavior.* New York: Henry Holt and Co., 1993.

Taylor, Walter K. *The Guide to Florida Wildflowers.* Dallas, Texas: Taylor Publishing Co., 1992.

Tiner, Ralph W. *Field Guide to Coastal Wetland Plants of the Southeastern United States.* Amherst, MA: The University of Massachusetts Press, 1993.

U.S. Dept. of Agriculture. *Plants for Coastal Dunes.* Washington. D.C.: U.S. Govt. Printing Office, 1984.

Van Atta, Marian. *Living Off the Land.* Melbourne, Florida: Geraventure Corp., 1973.

Van Atta, Marian. *Free Food from 27 Wild Edibles.* Melbourne, Florida: Geraventure Corp. and Great Outdoors Publishing Co., 1981.

Van Meter, Victoria B. *Florida's Sea Turtles.* Miami, Florida: Florida Power & Light Co., 1992.

Van Vleck, Sarita. *Ways of the Bird.* New York: Lyons & Burford, 1977.

Voss, Gilbert. *Seashore Life of Florida and the Caribbean.* Miami: Banyan Books, 1976.

Index

Why do mullet jump? Where do hermit crabs live? What's all that noise? Find out! Read...

The Nature of Florida's Waterways

Mangroves and manatees, oysters and ibis, ducks and dragonflies, turtles and tarpon:
There are *so* many fascinating creatures to be discovered along the waterfront!
Let Cathie Katz introduce you to them, and see how they're all connected by nature's web.

The Nature of Florida's Neighborhoods

is now available

This is a book for every Floridian and every visitor to Florida

Popular Florida wildlife author Cathie Katz has done it again—turned the mundane into magic!

Take a journey into the soul of Florida… bugs and all

What does a no-see-um look like?

Why do fire ants cause so much pain?

How can you keep squirrels out of your birdfeeders?

What's the difference between a honeybee and a bumblebee?

What's with those love bugs?

Are stink bugs all bad?

What's a poop bug?

Are bats dangerous?

The latest book in Cathie Katz' habitat series, *The Nature of Florida's Neighborhoods*, describes lizards, love bugs, cockroaches, backyard birds, wildflowers, slugs, moles, butterfly feeding, bedbugs, black widow spiders, rattlers, aphids, mole crickets, armadillos, caterpillars, house flies, recluse spiders, dandelions, possums, geckos, ants, crows, scrub jays, legless glass lizards, sparrows, chickadees, scorpions, bagworms, killer bees, lice, ticks, turkey vultures, woodpeckers, wasps, black-eyed Susans, weeds, Spanish moss, strangler figs.

67

The Nature of Florida's Ocean Life

By Cathie Katz

IS NOT ANOTHER SAVE-THE-WHALE BOOK

…It's about nurdles, turtles, bottles, sloppy guts, sea beans, Cuban rafts, lighthouses, comb jellies, sunken treasures, sea hares, LEGO® divers, pipefish, pansies, elvers, onion anemones, Sargasso Sea, mantis shrimp, gannets, coral gametes, sailfish, the Gulf Stream, upside down jellies, puffers, sand, sneakers, slugs, sea whips, the fastest fish in the Atlantic, water striders, sand dollars, plankters, algae, pearl fish, sea fans, plume worms, frog fish, octopodes, spirula, moray eels, lobster migration, sea weeds, gulls, whale lice, flounder larvae, chitons, flamingo tongues, sunfish, barracuda, Christmas tree worms, sea nettles, limpets, salps, oil blob fish, dead man's fingers, popeyed squids, frigatebirds, sea roaches, cleaner shrimp, sponges, ringed anemones, sargassum fish, sea walnuts, the most abundant bird in the world, sea cucumbers, pistol shrimp…

Simple Guide to Common Drift Seeds

Illustrations by Pamela Paradine and Cathie Katz

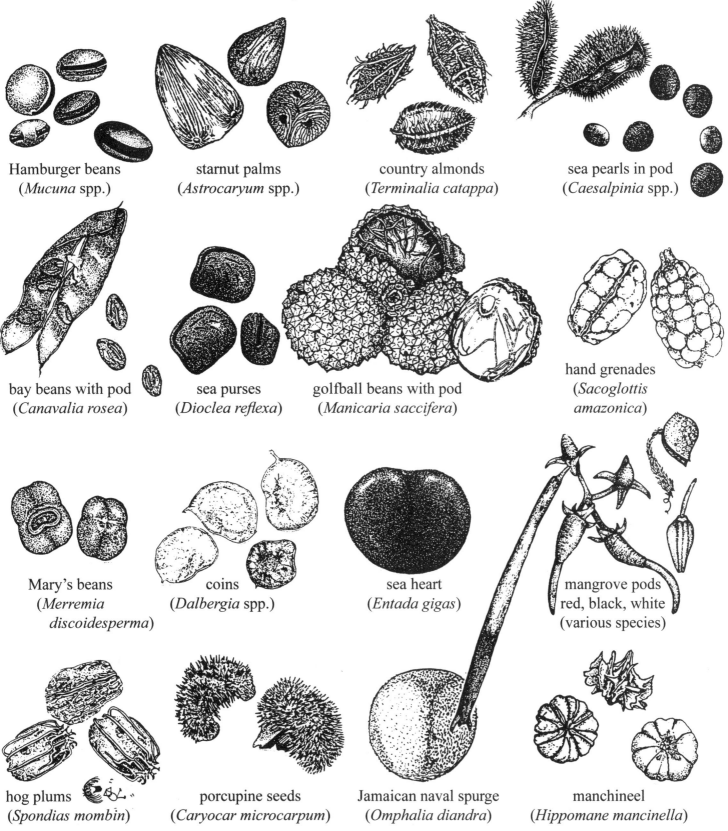

Hamburger beans
(*Mucuna* spp.)

starnut palms
(*Astrocaryum* spp.)

country almonds
(*Terminalia catappa*)

sea pearls in pod
(*Caesalpinia* spp.)

bay beans with pod
(*Canavalia rosea*)

sea purses
(*Dioclea reflexa*)

golfball beans with pod
(*Manicaria saccifera*)

hand grenades
(*Sacoglottis
amazonica*)

Mary's beans
(*Merremia
discoidesperma*)

coins
(*Dalbergia* spp.)

sea heart
(*Entada gigas*)

mangrove pods
red, black, white
(various species)

hog plums
(*Spondias mombin*)

porcupine seeds
(*Caryocar microcarpum*)

Jamaican naval spurge
(*Omphalia diandra*)

manchineel
(*Hippomane mancinella*)

About the Author

Cathie Katz was a world traveler and an eager student of the natural world. At various times she lived in Israel, Holland, Germany, Spain and Portugal. In 1983 she alighted near the Atlantic Ocean in Melbourne Beach, Florida. She became a senior editor at the Johns Hopkins University/Applied Physics Laboratory at Cape Canaveral Air Station. A superb wildlife illustrator, she began drawing the animals, plants and objects she observed on her frequent walks along the shoreline and became fascinated with sea beans in particular. Her interest spawned this, the first in a series of four Florida natural history books which were originally (quite successfully) self-published.

Cathie's inquiries into the world travels of sea beans led her to a collaboration with Dr. Charles R. Gunn. Together they founded *The Drifting Seed* newsletter and established an annual international symposium of sea bean enthusiasts that still meets in the Melbourne area. In 2000, Sierra Club Books published her illustrated diary *Nature, A Day at a Time: An Uncommon Look at Common Wildlife*. She also co-authored *The Little Book of Sea-Beans and Other Beach Treasures* with Dr. Ed Perry. Her unfinished last book, *Beaches and Beyond*, was to have been an illustrated book about the behaviors of ocean animals, showing that science and spirit are inseparable. Like her literary creation Little Larry, Cathie was an indomitable spirit and a gentle soul. Although she passed from this Earth in November, 2001, she has bequeathed her excitement and enthusiasm for the natural world to us through her books.

Notes

Notes

Notes

Notes